FORCES OF TAEKWONDO

New Revised Edition

2011

Fifteenth Edition

Library of Congress Gv 1114.3 .S44

©Copyright 1979

by Edward B. Sell and Brenda J. Sell

Copyright material for publications. No implied permission shall be assumed for rights to reproduce any part of the book totally or partially by any means electronically or mechanically, including photocopying, recording, mimeograph or any information or storage retrieval system without the expressed written consent from publisher and author.

United States Chung Do Kwan Association, Inc.

Edward B. Sell and Brenda J. Sell

P.O. Box 1474 Lakeland Fl. 33802 Phone (863) 858-9427

Fax (863) 858-4437 http.www.uscdka.com

DEDICATION

For more than forty-four years, I thought I was happy and secure because of all that "I" have done for myself. By investing all of my adult life into this martial art, I thought that was the way to find true "peace". I was wrong. There is only one way to find peace and that is through God. The Bible tells of such peace in Phillipians chapter 4 verses 6 and 7 (reading from the Living Bible version) it says: "Don't worry about anything; instead, pray about everything; tell God your needs and don't forget to thank Him for His answers. If you do this you will experience God's peace, which is far more wonderful than the human mind can understand. His peace will keep your thoughts and your hearts quiet and at rest as you trust in Christ Jesus." I wish to dedicate this book, the United States Chung Do Kwan Association and all my Taekwondo efforts to my Lord and Saviour Jesus Christ. For it is by His long suffering, death and resurrection, that my soul is saved and at peace with God.

This is our prayer:
As you meditate upon these words, you will desire to seek the Lord as we have, and recieve his blessings as we have, through our Lord and Savior, Jesus Christ.

> For the Lord God is a sun and shield: the Lord will give grace and glory: no good thing will he withhold from them that walk uprightly.
>
> O Lord of hosts, blessed is the man that trusteth in thee.
>
> Psalms 84:11,12

The authors:

Grandmaster Edward B. Sell

Grandmaster Brenda J. Sell

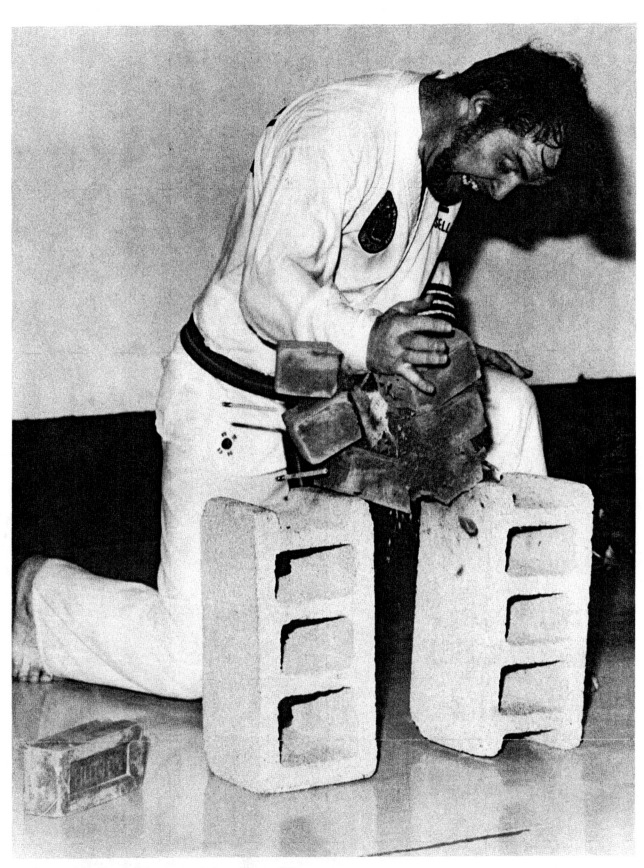

Grandmaster Sell smashes three housebricks, demonstrating the *POWER* of Taekwondo Chung Do Kwan. Photo taken in 1973.

Martial TAEKWONDO Times
Fitness & Health

WORLDWIDE COVERAGE SINCE 1980

BRENDA J. SELL
This Lady is a Grandmaster!

SUCCESSFUL JOINT LOCKS
Street-Wise Techniques That are Quick, Safe & Effective!

STRIKE FIRST!
When TKD Philosophy Is not the Wisest Course

WHITE TIGER CUT POWDER
Alternative to Western Medicine

FRONT KICK: THE NATURAL WAY
Grm. Kim Soo's Chayon-Ryu Principles of Balance, Rhythm, Breathing, & Alignment

QUEST FOR CAMELOT
Meet the Martial Artists Behind the Characters

TOUR KOREA
Armchair View

PLUS:
Romance in the Dojang
Training to be a Loser

OCT 1998 $3.25
CAN $3.65
U.K. £2.20

Visit us at **taekwondotimes.com**

Grandmaster Sell and his instructor, Grandmaster Hae Man Park, 10th Degree Black Belt from the World Chung Do Kwan Headquarters and the Kukkiwon, Seoul, Korea. Photo taken 1973.

KUKKIWON
WORLD TAEKWONDO HEADQUARTERS

#635 Yuksam-dong, Gangnam-gu
Seoul, Korea(Postal Code :135-908)
http://www.kukkiwon.or.kr

TEL. 82-2-563-3339
FAX. 82-2-552-3025

May 07. 2009.

As a president of the World Taekwondo Headquarters, Kukkiwon, I am very pleased to recommend <u>Forces of Taekwondo</u> written by one of our very dedicated and loyal American Masters, Edward B. Sell.

Mr. Sell has been a pioneer of modern day Taekwondo since he began his training in the early 60's while stationed at Osan Air Force Base, near Seoul, Korea. His enthusiasm and contribution to Taekwondo has been instrumental in the development of Taekwondo in the United States. The Kukkiwon, World Taekwondo Headquarters recognizes him as an International Master since 1972, American Coach for the U.S. National Team at the 1st World Taekwondo Championships held in Seoul 1973, an International Referee since 1974 and a forerunner in Taekwondo education through writing and publishing many Taekwondo training manuals since 1968. The Kukkiwon and World Taekwondo Federation have awarded him several merit awards for his life-long contributions.

He has trained thousands of Taekwondo practitioners to become Black Belt qualified. One of his most accomplished achievements was in 2001, when he appeared in front of the Kukkiwon World Taekwondo Headquarters Black Belt Dan Examination Board and successfully passed the test for the 9th Dan. He was the first foreigner (Non-Asian) ever to do so.

I have personally supported Mr. Sell in his Taekwondo career for almost 50 years. This publication is authenticated by his many years of hard training and dedicated research plus the approval, support and accreditation of this office.

I am very confident that this book will provide the readers with much useful information and abundant illustrations on theoretical, practical and spiritual aspects of Taekwondo in it's truest form, I place my personal recommendation.

Woon Kyu Uhm
President
Kukkiwon

ABOUT THE AUTHORS

EDWARD B. SELL

Grandmaster Edward B. Sell is the highest ranked non-oriental in the world in Taekwondo. His credentials (held with the World Taekwondo Federation and the World Chung Do Kwan Association) and reputation are world renown. Grandmaster Sell has received the highest recognition, appointments, and degree of anyone outside of Korea. He is a 9th Degree Black Belt (August, 1997). He is also the author of America's first Taekwondo training manual. At the time of publication, Grandmaster Sell has more than 40 years of experience in the study, training, researching, and teaching of one of the World's most effective forms of self defense. He is an International Master and Official, the first American to receive International Referee Certification in Korea, 1974. He is Founding President of the following: U.S. Chung Do Kwan Association, Korean Taekwondo Association of America, Taekwondo Rangers, Christian Taekwondo University and the Sell Team (International Christian Demonstration Team). He and his team travel worldwide by invitation of the United States Military Chaplains Dept. enouraging troops to "Be all they can be." He was the Coach of the U.S. Team in the 1st World Taekwondo Championship, Korea, 1973, and Master Instructor in Policemen's Combative Tactics. He was also United States Air Force Combative Measures Instructor from 1960-1967. He has promoted more than 5,000 Black Belts in his career and his teaching principles have been exposed to nearly 250,000 American students.

A UNIQUE HUSBAND & WIFE BLACK BELT TEAM

BRENDA J. SELL

Grandmaster Brenda J. Sell started her Taekwondo training at the age of 14. Throughout her training, she has accumulated innumerable trophies and awards in both Sparring and Forms Competition on local, state, and national levels. Her powerful round kick and lightning fast reverse punch brought her many titles. Today she is an 8th Degree Black Belt and an expert in all areas of teaching Taekwondo. "Grandmaster Brenda" received her official title as the first woman to test for the 8th Degree in March 2003 by Grandmaster Hae Man Park. In 1998 she was awarded the position of the first female Grandmaster. In 1997 she was inducted into the Hall of Fame. In 1989 she received a Letter of Citation from the WTF President Un Yong Kim, and was named USCDKA Black Belt of the Decade. In 1977 she became the first female in the world to receive International Referee credentials from the World Taekwondo Federation (WTF). On April 16, 2004 she became the President of the United States Chung Do Kwan Association and Evangelistic Taekwondo Exhibitions, Inc. She continues to be a forerunner of female students and takes special interest in the development of Taekwondo training aides, helping people to discover their gifts and talents, teaching and motivation of children.

Grandmaster Brenda is the National Forms Coordinator and teaches seminars across the country on ways to improve forms. She is the first female grandmaster in the art and science of Taekwondo Chung Do Kwan.

A Note From Grandmaster Sell

In 1967 I made the choice to become one of America's first professional Taekwondo Instructors. I guess I can be considered one of the first successful pioneers in the martial arts industry. I have always tried to uphold the values, traditions and authenticity of Taekwondo as an art, science and sport. The contents of this textbook are documented proof that an American can indeed become a Master Instructor and yes, even a Grandmaster.

Without hesitation, I give credit to the original founders an promoters of Taekwondo: the Korean-born, Korean trained, Korean Master Instructors. But, let's face facts; this is America, and our language and culture are much different. Therefore, the training of an American must be modified. To modify this martial art without sacrificing effectiveness, and to formulate a profession, has taken much patience and many years of research. For those who are not members of the United States Chung Do Kwan Association, we hope this textbook will stimulate an interest to join our elite martial arts organization. After the many years that I have dedicated to this one style of Taekwondo, I feel that I have only scratched the surface of the many rewards, benefits an strengths that can be obtained. After reading this book, I sincerely hope that you will have been enlightened to this "Art and Science" that I have found to be a unique way to strengthen the physical and spiritual man within all of us.

March 24, 1995

Table of Contents

Chapter One: Introduction to Taekwondo *1*
   Origin and History 6
   Weapons of Taekwondo 12
   Basic Stances 16
   Basic Korean Terminology 21
   Rules and Regulations 23
   Customs and Courtesies 25

Chapter Two: Profiles of an American Master *29*
   What is a Master 31
   The Kwan' Jang 33
   The Whole Man 49

Chapter Three: Six Parts of a Taekwondo Class *57*
   Stretching Exercises (Part One) 59
   Techniques/Fundamentals (Part Two) 63
   Forms/Poomse, Taegeuk Forms (Part Three) 84
   One Step Sparring, 1- 20 (Part Four) 104
   Free Sparring (Part Five) 117
   Calisthenics (Part Six) 122

Chapter Four: Sparring and Self Defense *123*
   What is a Fake 124
   Basic Blocking Techniques 126
   Taekwondo as a Form of Self Defense 130
   Vulnerable Areas of the Body 135
   Defense Against Weapons of the Street 136

Chapter Five: U.S. Chung Do Kwan Association *137*
   Patches, Emblems & Logos 138
   History 140
   USCDKA Timeline 143
   Ranking System 152
   Testing Requirements, Student Ranks 153

Chapter Six: Women in Taekwondo *175*
   Basic Self Defense for Women 179
   The World's Oldest Social Crime 195

Chapter Seven: The Art of Demonstrating *203*
   Breaking Boards, Concrete Slabs, and Bricks 206

Chapter Eight: Tae Kwon Do, The Sport *221*
   History of Tournaments 222
   Tournament Strategies 238

A Final Thought: Developing The Spirit Man *253*

CREDITS

We wish to thank all those who have contributed both directly and indirectly to the publication of this book. Everyday we are learning more through giving of ourselves to our Taekwondo family. Without you, there would be no reason to write this book. The faithful and committed members of the U.S. Chung Do Kwan Association are one of our most valuable assets. Thank you for placing your trust and confidence in us as your leaders.

Listed below are a few of those who have been an exceptional help or support. Thank you for helping us to document the decades of experience and knowledge to share with others who are on a Quest to be their Best in the art and science of Taekwondo.

Master Keith Lohse
Chief Master Bernie Fritts
Grandmaster James Covensky
Grandmaster Keith Hafner
Grandmaster Robert Smith
Grandmaster Mark Begley
Professor Carol Covensky
Rev. Wayne Friedt
Ernest & Wilma Begley
Chief Instructor Sally Ax
Master Barbara Murphy
Head Master Robby Sell

THE PURPOSE OF THIS TEXTBOOK

If you read this textbook often, and memorize what you read, you will soon discover that you will develop great insight while beginning to understand this fantastic "Art." The "Science" of Taekwondo will come to you as you continue your training and learn how to shift your body weight and focus power as you move with your hand or foot.

Use this textbook as your silent instructor when you are away from your formal class session or training area.

Attempt to duplicate the moves and techniques of the instructors pictured in this textbook and you will have taken a giant step forward toward meeting the requirements necessary for you to advance in the "art and Science" of Taekwondo Chung Do Kwan.

By using this textbook wisely, you will find yourself on a smoother path toward the goal of attaining the Black Belt. As a student of Taekwondo you will have the opportunity to become a healthier, more disciplined individual through dedicated study and practice.

It is the ultimate goal of he United States Chung Do Kwan Association, through each Black Belt Instructor and this textbook, to teach you to the most up to date training methods in order to give you the keys to becoming a whole person: to be strong in mind, body, and spirit.

Our motto says it all:
To give strength to the weak,
Confidence to the timid, and
Spiritual guidance to those who seek after God.

INTRODUCTION TO TAE KWON DO

TAE

"To Strike with Foot"

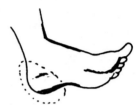

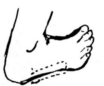

KWON

"To Strike with Hand"

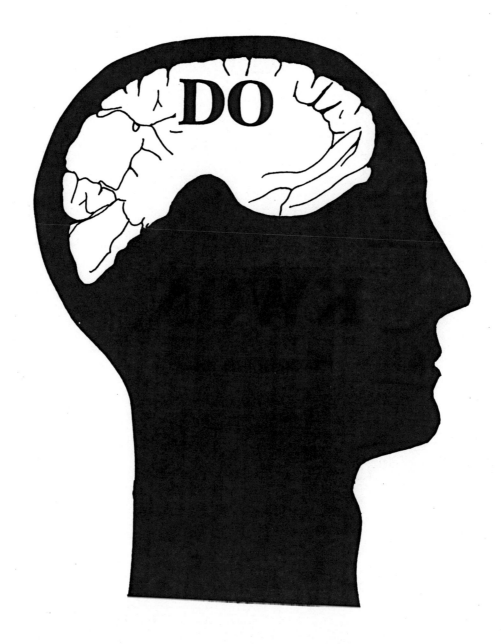

"The way, the confidence, the knowledge, the common sense and intelligence never to misuse this ancient form of self defense."

"What Is TaeKwonDo?"

Origin of Word: South Korea

Ancient Definition: A form of martial art that dates back to 37 years before the birth of Christ, using the bare hands and feet as weapons against enemies, with emphasis on kicking techniques. A forerunner of modern-day Korean Karate.

Modern-Day Definition: After 2,000 years of research, beginning with the warriors of the ancient orient (Korea); passed down from father to son; from Master to Korean student; from Korean Master to American student; from American Master to American student. All practitioners have found ways to improve and apply the many benefits of becoming proficient in one of the world's most effective forms of hand and foot fighting, and at the same time, have discovered many ways to improve one's character, self confidence, self esteem and physical fitness.

Breaking the word into three parts: TAE refers to kicking into the vulnerable areas of an assailant; KWON refers to striking with the hand into the vulnerable areas of an assailant; DO refers to "the way," a method through which one can find self-confidence and "peace of mind."

As a World Sport: Through the formation of the World TaeKwonDo Federation (WTF), founded in 1973, World Masters have created a unique competitive sport with a surprisingly limited incidence of bodily injury. Protective body armor, such as chest protectors and groin protectors, plus strict rules, have made one of the World's most powerful and effective Martial Arts into a "Modern-Day Gladiator's Sports Spectacular Event." One must witness a World Championship event in order to experience the impact not experienced by any other body contact sport.

This mural painting, depicting two men practicing a sort of TaeKwonDo, is drawn on the ceiling of Muyong-chong, a royal tomb of the Koguryo dynasty. The tomb in southern Manchuria is believed to have been built between 3 A.D. and 427 A.D. and was excavated by a group of archeologists in 1935.

THE ORIGIN AND HISTORY OF TAE KWON DO

From 660 A.D. to 892 A.D., the Dynasty of Silla reigned in the peninsula of Koryo, an area known today as Korea, located just south of China. To defend their kingdom against the constant harrassments and periodic invasions of their powerful northern neighbors, Chin Heung, the 24th King of Silla, formed an Officers Warrior Corps and named it "Hwa Rang Dan." To develop a superior method of self-defense, these ancient Korean warriors traveled to the mountains, forest and seashores of Koryo, studying the fighting habits of wild animals. From these animals, they sought to isolate those defensive and offensive techniques which gave each its most formidable advantage. These new techniques were then adapted to, and combined with, the traditional methods of self-defense. By incorporating the strict discipline taught by the Buddhist monks, particularly the rigorous exercises designed to develop intense concentration, these young warriors formulated the means to coordinate the mind and body into one harmonious system. This system was called "Soo Bak Do" or "Tae Kyun," meaning "The art of systematically kicking and punching with the bare feet and hands." This system rapidly became the most effective unarmed martial art in the world. The Hwa Rang Dan warrior, also known as the Subak Warrior, became renowned for his courage and skill in combat. Their legendary heroism inspired the people of Silla to rise and eventually conquer their enemies. With Silla's many victories, the peninsula of Koryo was united as one country for the first time in history. This defense and consolidation of the Kingdom of Silla, occurring 1400 years ago, is the most dramatic example in ancient history of the powerful impact of "hand and foot fighting." This is not to indicate, however, that the history of TaeKwonDo begins with the Dynasty of Silla. There are traces of TaeKwonDo as far back as 37 B.C. in the form of murals and giant carvings, pieces of art that were created during the Koguryo era.

Soo Bak Do retained its popularity through the Silla and Koryo dynasties and achieved its greatest prominence during the succeeding dynasty, which was established in 935 A.D. and ruled for 457 years. It was from the Koryo dynasty that the peninsula gained its modern name, Korea. The kingdom under these rulers was strictly militaristic in spirit, a fact dictated by the necessity of defending the country against continual foreign invasions. The soldiers of the Koryo dynasty were among the finest the country has ever produced, and their martial spirit and bravery has been a source of inspiration ever since. At this time, Soo Bak Do was practiced not only as a martial art, but also as a means to improve health and a sport to enjoy competitively. An extract from the historical record of Koryo says that "King Uijong admired the excellence of Yi Ui-min in (the sport of) Soo Bak and promoted him to a much higher military rank." With the rise of the Yi dynasty in Korea, founded by Yi Sung Kye in 1392, Soo Bak Do, which had been the special province of the military society during the Koryo period, became more popular as a national sport among the general public. Those who wanted to be employed by the military department of the royal government had to learn Soo Bak Do, since it became part of the test given to the applicants. During this time, King Chongjo published an illustrated textbook on the martial arts which included a major study of Soo Bak Do as one of the most effective means of unarmed self-defense. Except for internal political struggles, the last period of the Yi dynasty was an era of relative peace. This security and stability prompted a rise in the "peaceful arts," such as painting and literature, and a decline in the martial arts. Consequently, Soo Bak Do declined in general popularity and became the pastime of a few devotees, mainly young persons. It was at this point that the tradition of passing TaeKwonDo from father to son developed.

From the Sino-Japanese War of 1894 through World War II, Korea was involved in the continual military conflicts between China and Japan. During this period, these foreign fighting styles influenced Soo Bak Do practitioners. Teachers began to modernize their training methods. It was at this time that many teachers took it upon themselves to develop and organize training schools, called "toe'chongs" or "do'changs" using many names to promote their methods of teaching, such as Tae Soo Do, Tang Soo Do, Tae Kyun, Chong Do, Soo Bak, Tung Soo, Mu Do, Ji Do, Sang Do, Kang Do, plus many more. All of these Korean martial arts schools were classified as a "Kwan." After many years only the stronger ones survived. In 1945, after the liberation of South Korea, a number of martial arts teachers began a conscientious effort to revitalize the art of Taekwondo as a national sport, and also began to combine the ancient philosophical training into a modern method of self-defense, but also strengthened the mind as well as the body.

By 1950, there were 17 different styles of this Korean martial art. Each style embodied the same basic principles but were labeled by different names, many of which contradicted the others. It was not until 1961 that the Korean Government decided that something had to be done to preserve its national heritage in the field of martial arts. Much confusion was being spread throughout the world as each martial arts instructor left Korea claiming that his style was the best form of self-defense known to mankind. With the influence of high ranking government officials and the cooperation of prominent Taekwondo masters, the Korean Tae Kwon Do Association was formed in 1965. A program was then instituted by the Korean government to select those schools which best exemplified the tradition of Taekwondo. After much research, and an intense testing and reclassification of instructors, five schools were selected from the seventeen Korean styles to be charter members of the

Korean TaeKwonDo Association. Since that time, four other styles have been recognized as members of the worlds first and strongest TaeKwonDo Association.

During this transitional period, the author was stationed with the U.S. Air Force at Osan Air Base and was training at the local Chung Do Kwan school in Pyon Teak-kun (central South Korea). He well remembers the confusion that overwhelmed the ranks of the Korean instructors. He also remembers his Korean instructors coming back from Seoul City battered and bruised after being re-evaluated and accepted as members into the new association. He often wondered what their opponents looked like after being told that his instructors received good grades while being tested for their sparring ability.

In 1973, the Korean TaeKwonDo Association organized and sponsored the First World TaeKwonDo Championship, held in Seoul, Korea at a site designated as the World Headquarters for TaeKwonDo called the "Kukkiwon". The Kukkiwon is a massive stadium built by the Korean government for the study, research, and handling of all the administrative affairs of TaeKwonDo throughout the world. In May, 1973, twenty countries formed the World TaeKwonDo Federation and officially made the Kukkiwon their headquarters. From that time, TaeKwonDo has rapidly spread around the world, not only as a unique martial art but as a fascinating competitive sport.

Nine foot tall statue of Subak Warriors in Sokkuran Cave in Kyungn, Korea (37 B.C.)

Delegates at the organizing conference of the World Taekwondo Federation at Kukkiwon 28th May 1973

Kukkiwon (World Taekwondo Center)

Headquarters of the World Taekwondo Federation.

KARATE

China's Influence: Ancient oriental history tells us that both Japanese and Korean cultures originated in Old China. Both countries still use ancient Chinese lettering, very similar to our Old English script that we use on official documents. When we analyze the word Karate we find that it consists of two ancient Chinese words: "kara" meaning empty and "te" meaning hand. Another translation is: "Old China technique". Because of the many wars and dictatorships which attempted to eliminate various cultures throughout the oriental countries of the Far East, there are no authentic documents stating exactly where the methods of "hand and foot fighting" actually originated. Within this training manual the author tries his best to simplify this history and illustrate the theories and teaching technology using the most modern methods that have proven to be successful while teaching thousands of English speaking students.

Actually, the word Karate comes from the Japanese language. The Japanese originally introduced the oriental form of hand and foot fighting to the United States, therefore the word karate has had at least a ten to fifteen year head start in the English speaking language. Karate is a word that can be found in most modern English dictionaries. When the word karate is used in this book, the author speaks of hand and foot fighting styles in general and he is not emphasizing one particular style of martial art. At this point it is very important that the reader understand this fact.

Karate as a Form of Self Defense: Originally karate was a system of self defense, however in recent decades karate has been transformed into a form of recreation, a sport, and a form of physical fitness. Self defense is still a vital part of karate training, unlike most other sports where students or practitioners are taught to compete entirely against opponents of identical or very similar training. Students of karate are trained to fight against many other combative systems such as defense against various restraint holds (grabs), and defensive tactics against weapons that may be used by street fighting thugs. Men, women, boys, and girls of all ages find karate to be a very exciting and simplified method of learning how to defend themselves and at the same time discover it to be a unique system to keep physically fit. Such training is absolutely unique and cannot be found in any other form of martial art. For example, boxers are taught to fight boxers, and wrestlers are trained to wrestle. What could they hope to do if attacked by some maniac weilding a knife, broken bottle or club, or find themselves confronted with a pistol thrust into their face, or attacked from behind unexpectedly? A well trained karate student may be able to save his own life and the lives of others since he may be highly skilled or have the expertise in the use of both hands and feet and be able to unleash countless striking methods using the secret of "focused power," which is also capable of penetrating solid wooden boards and smashing concrete slabs with one blow.

WHERE DO YOU FIND TAEKWONDO?

TaeKwonDo (Korean Karate) can be found in most states and is growing very rapidly as millions of Americans and foreigners alike are realizing that this mysterious martial art is a very satisfying way to release the tensions and pressures of home, work and office through the disciplined teachings, relaxed atmosphere and the brotherhood from fellow students.

Most training centers are in commercial buildings, where the majority of professional Masters practice and teach. The recreation department of your city may have a TaeKwonDo program in which a part-time instructor teaches two to three times per week. The YMCA and other sports minded associations may also carry TaeKwonDo programs.

The training area required for TaeKwonDo is simply open space in an area at least 20' x 60' for a group class. Other necessary equipment for training include a striking bag and a stretch bar. Mats are not necessary for TaeKwonDo class sessions since there usually is no throwing or falling to the ground during practice.

FACTS ABOUT TAEKWONDO & KARATE

There are many rumors that have been around since martial arts has been introduced to this country. Below are just a few of the facts that may help those who have been misdirected by some of the false statements.

1. A Black Belt does not register his hands as a lethal weapon.
2. A Black Belt does not show his credentials before fighting an assailant.
3. A Black Belt does not need to announce that he is a Black Belt before defending himself.
4. A Black Belt does not need to have calluses on his hands.
5. A Black Belt does not break his fingers and make them all even.
6. A Black Belt does not scream and shout like a maniac before striking an assailant.
7. A Black Belt does not need to be a male.
8. A Black Belt should not be a violent person.
9. A Black Belt does not need to be over the age of 18.
10. A Black Belt does not always break boards and bricks to prove his skills.

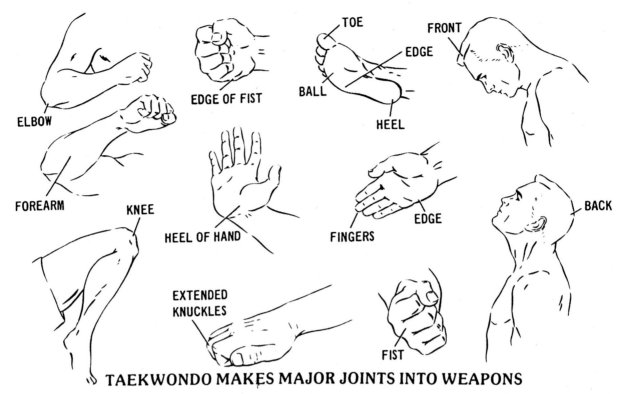

TAEKWONDO MAKES MAJOR JOINTS INTO WEAPONS

TaeKwonDo can turn important joints of the body into weapons so that one can utilize his skills to defend himself from the unexpected attack of an assailant, and also to fight for the defense of loved ones and country. Fists turn into hammers, fingertips to sharp spearheads, the edge of the palm to a knife blade; feet can have the effects of huge iron hammers. To create such effects, there are basic ways to turn the fists, hands, legs and feet into weapons, and certain fundamental actions to move these weapons. There are various forms and patterns of movement to swiftly connect sequences of actions that move the weapons to the right or left, foreward or backward, both defensively and offensively. There are one-step prearranged sequences of blocking, thrusting, kicking, and striking with the hand using systemmatic counter-attacking methods unlike any known to the average man.

After the fundamental, prearranged sequences of actions are mastered thoroughly, students are ready to learn the "ultimate of TaeKwonDo training" called "Free Style Sparring," which means that the students strike and kick at each other using specific TaeKwonDo techniques. The U.S. Chung Do Kwan Association has several types of free style sparring: no contact, light or controlled contact, precision sparring, and full contact using protective gear and tournament sparring with and without protective gear. With time, the student can rise through the many types and levels of sparring at his own will. In national and world competitions specific rules are enforced that place the face and head "off limits" to any hand technique and the contestants wear body armour (chest protectors) since full contact is implied. Only qualified Black Belts are eligible to compete in such events.

TaeKwonDo is a sport so powerful that it is dangerous to experiment with its effectiveness upon a person, so experts demonstrate it upon bricks and wooden boards, proving the devastating power sent forth through the limbs of the human body when applying the principles of one of the world's oldest forms of self-defense.

PERSONAL WEAPONS

These are the parts of the body which can be used for self-defense and counterattack. Developing skill in the use of your personal weapons should enable you to successfully defend yourself when attacked.

1. The Head.--The front and back of the head are quite substantial and can be used for butting.

2. The Hand.--When using the hand as a weapon, the wrist should be held straight for all blows except the "heel-of-hand" blow. In addition to regular "closed-fist" blows, you can also strike with the "edge-of-hand" and the "edge-of-fist." These two blows are most effective when delivered with a chopping motion from across the body (from the inside to the outside) with the palm down, or downward with the palm facing in. Blows delivered from across the body permit the use of the large trunk muscles. When used correctly, these muscles add considerable speed and force to the blow. The "heel-of-hand" blow is delivered upward when you are close to your opponent. The fingers must be flexed slightly and held rigid for the "finger-jab." The "extended-knuckles" blow requires the thumb to be held firmly against the index finger, thereby helping to "firm-up" the hand.

3. The Elbow.--When used as a weapon, the elbow should be fully flexed. The most effective blow is delivered toward the rear. This is probably the most powerful blow the average person can deliver. A forearm or elbow blow can also be thrown by raising the arm about shoulder high, flexing the elbow, and then swinging the arm forward toward the inside.

4. The Knee.--"Knee-lifts" to the face and groin can be very effective when executed properly. The knee should be flexed fully by pulling the foot back as close to the buttocks as possible, as the knee is raised. The "knee-lift" and all other kicks must be executed quickly, followed by an immediate return to a strong, balanced position.

5. The Foot.--The toe of the foot is used in kicking forward; the edge, ball, and heel are used sideward. The ball and heel are used in kicking backward, and the heel is used in stamping. To execute a kick properly, you must first flex the hip. This is accomplished by raising the knee until the thigh is parallel to the floor. The lower leg is then "snapped" or "thrust" out to complete the kick. A short, snappy kick using the forward foot is extremely effective when directed against the opponent's shin, knee, or groin.

THE PROPER FIST

The fist is the most common weapon used in the Asian fighting arts. Striking with the first two knuckles when punching or when applying the very fast "back fist strike" it is very important to roll the fingers tightly and lock the thumb over the first two fore fingers; next the students must remember to lock the wrist so that the top of the fist is even in line with the forearm and the second or center knuckle is "centered" in the middle of the fist or in line with an imaginary line down the center of the arm (this line passes between the first and second knuckle). It is a fact that 98% of men and women in this country do not know how to make a fist properly. Thus the majority of injuries (in a non-trained person) occur with broken bones in the hand after a street confrontation.

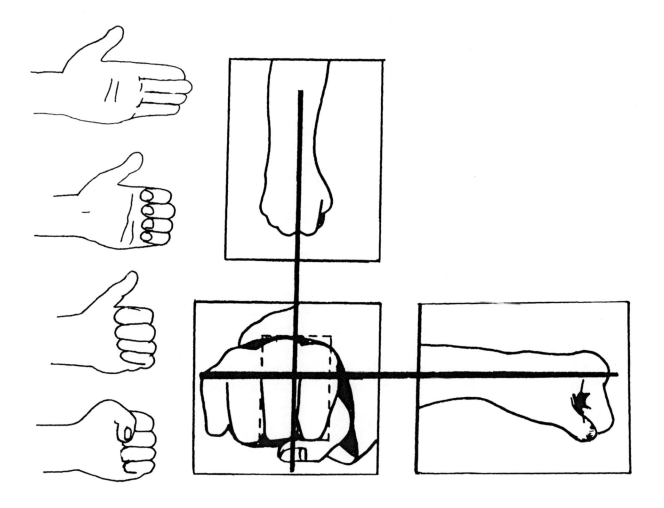

Blocking techniques are introduced to the beginners at their first class session.

BLOCKING WEAPONS & TECHNIQUES

1. Outside edge of hand (suto)
2. Inside edge of hand (ridge-hand)
3. Inside fore-arm
4. Outside fore-arm
5. Top of fore-arm
6. Palm of hand
7. Back of hand
8. Elbow
9. Knee
10. Shin
11. Bottom of instep
12. Side of foot
13. Ball of foot
14. Shoulder
15. Hip

STRIKING WEAPONS

1. Suto
2. Ridge-hand
3. Spear-hand
4. Two finger spear
5. One finger spear
6. Four knuckle punch
7. Two knuckle punch
8. One knuckle punch
9. Ox-jaw
10. Hammer blow
11. Fore fist
12. Back fist
13. Back hand
14. Bear's claw
15. Tiger's mouth
16. Thumb thrust
17. Palm strike
18. Knee
19. Top of foot
20. Ball of foot
21. Heel of foot
22. Side of foot
23. Head
24. Elbow
25. Forehead
26. Back of head

SIX BASIC STANCE POSITIONS

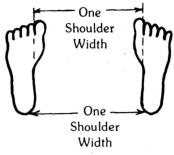

Chim'bee Stance

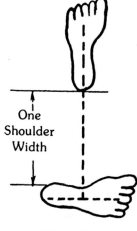

"T" Stance

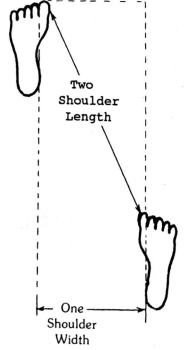

Square Stance

Note: The "Walking Stance" also called a "Short Square Stance" is not considered an additional stance, but a modified version of the formal square stance.

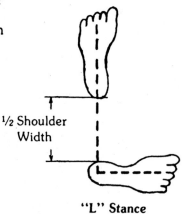

"L" Stance

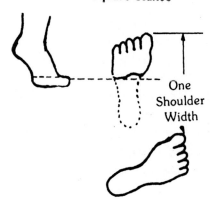

Tiger Stance

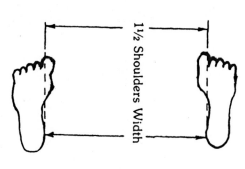

Straddle Stance

Duplicate these stances while looking down at your feet.

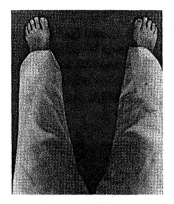

Chimbee stance

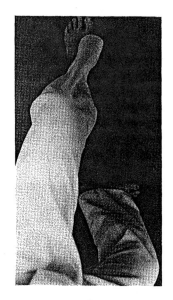

T-stance

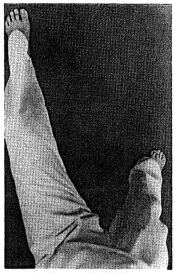

Square stance

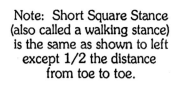

Note: Short Square Stance (also called a walking stance) is the same as shown to left except 1/2 the distance from toe to toe.

L-stance

Tiger Stance

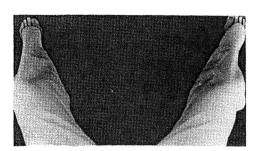

Straddle stance

WHY BARE FEET?

Reasons for not wearing shoes while practicing martial arts: 1) To create "natural" body balance and co-ordination. Note: We were not born wearing shoes. 2) Ancient Oriental Custom. It is said that shoes bring in the troubles of the street. When visiting a friend in the Orient, one does not bring him the troubles of the street or one's own personal problems, but to visit another's home means to pay him and his family the respect and to hear what he may have to say. 3) Prevention of injury from the hard leather shoe while sparring with a fellow student. 4) A method to keep the training area clean from pebbles and dirt from the street. 5) A method to strengthen and condition the feet and ankles.

BOWING

1   2   3

What does it mean when a student bows? To bow is to show respect and humility. This ancient custom dates back to the beginning of time, when one man first approached another man in friendship and wanted to show respect for one another's presence. When a martial arts student and his instructor bow to each other they are showing respect. When one student bows to another, they are showing respect and friendship towards each other. When students bow to the American flag at the beginning and end of class, they are saluting the flag and honoring what it represents. If the Korean flag is on display, they show their respect by bowing to it in recognition of the fact that Korea is the mother country of Taekwondo. The bow can also be compared to the American handshake or the military salute.

TWO TYPES OF BOWING

<u>Respectful Bow:</u> Student comes to attention, with cupped hands at his sides. The bow is then made at least at a forty-five degree angle, with the face looking at the floor, then slowly back upward to attention. *Photo #2*

<u>Challenging Bow:</u> Student comes to attention with clenched fists at sides, looking straight into his oppont's face while the bow is made at about a thirty degree angle, then back to the attention position. This type of bow is used primarily for one-step spar, free style spar, and when competing in tournaments. *Note: it would be considered disrespectful to use the challenging bow when addressing your instructor, a Black Belt or higher ranked student.*
Photo #3

CHIM'BEE [Ready]

Other than the position of attention, chim'bee is the very first TaeKwonDo Karate stance that a beginning student is taught. It is indeed a very important stance and has much meaning. The author refers to it as a "conscious self hypnosis" in which the student voluntarily places himself as he prepares to receive the formalities of TaeKwonDo. It is in this position that the student begins and completes his formal training prior to being placed in the "at ease" position. All forms and styles of karate have a similar stance. When properly translated, Chim'bee means ready. This Korean word may also be pronounced as "Joon'bi". As you continue to read through this book, the author tries his best to spell the Korean or Japanese word phonetically as it should be pronounced, therefore the spelling may differ from other sourcebooks.

Shoulders thrown back; chest out; stomach in; knees locked; feet exactly one shoulder width toe to toe and heel to heel; tight fists forming an upside down "V" just below the beltline; straight/sober facial expression.

BASIC KOREAN TERMINOLOGY

NOTE: Throughout this manual the author has spelled many of the Korean words phonetically, assuming this will aid the student in proper pronunciation. The same words or terms may be spelled differently in other training material.

A. COMMANDS

1. Che-dee-yet . . . . Attention
2. Kyoung-yet . . . . Bow
3. Chim-bee . . . . Ready Position
4. Pa-doe . . . . Return to ready position
5. Tol-dah-sult . . . . About face
6. Shult . . . . At ease
7. Yuk-jin-shult . . . . Parade rest
8. Ahn-jo . . . . Please sit down
9. Eden-nult . . . . Please stand up
10. Toro . . . . Turn toward Instructor
11. Com-mult . . . . Line up and adjust uniform
12. Gi-yup . . . . Shout of enthusiasm

B. NAMES

1. Toe-balk . . . . Training uniform
   (sometimes spelled as Doe-balk)
2. Toe-chong . . . . Training area
   (sometimes spelled as Doe-chang)
3. Tae Kwon Do (pronounced doe) . . . . The "ART" of empty hand & foot fighting
   (sometimes spelled as one word)
4. Karate (Japanese term) . . . . Empty hand fighting
5. Kung-fu (Chinese term, Kong-fu) . . A gentle form of Karate practiced in China
6. Chung Do Kwan . . . . One of the original nine training systems used to teach Korean Karate
7. Kata (Japanese term) . . . . Patterns of defensive movements which must be memorized in order to strengthen the mind & body, speed reflexes and program the student's instinct to block & counter attack.
8. Poom'se . . . . Korean term for "forms"

9. Eel-bon-da-dee-un . . . . One step spar or semi spar, a training technique used to sharpen the students' countering ability

10. Numbers (counting):
    #1. = Hona, 1st = il
    #2. = Dul, 2nd = ee
    #3. = saht, 3rd = som
    #4. = naht, 4th = sa
    #5. = tul'sult, 5th = oh
    #6. = yul'sult, 6th = yuk
    #7. = eel'gulp, 7th = chil
    #8. = yul'dul, 8th = pil
    #9. = ah'hoop, 9th = goo
    #10. = yul, 10th = ship

C. Proper terms used when referring to rank (skill level) within the Martial Arts:

1. Gup.. (also spelled Geup) . . . . . Student Rank. A classification of a student's proficiency in Tae Kwon Do
2. Kyu (Japanese term) . . . . Exactly the same meaning as "gup," but used in the teaching of a Japanese Martial Art.
   Note: not used in TaeKwon Do
3. Dee . . . . The "Belt", which is the symbol of one's rank.
4. Dan (pronounced as don) . . . . A degree of proficiency within the Black Belt ranks

RULES & REGULATIONS

WITHIN THE TOE'CHONG (TAE KWON DO TRAINING AREA)

1. When entering the Training Area:
   A. Remove shoes before stepping onto the floor. There are several reasons for removing your shoes.
      1. Keep the floor clean.
      2. Oriental philosophy states that by removing your shoes you are leaving your problems on the outside, thereby giving you a clear head when on the training floor.
      3. To prevent injuries while practicing TaeKwonDo.
      4. To create better body balance with the bare feet and to improve coordination.
   B. Bow before entering and when leaving.
   C. Bow to the Instructor or Senior Black Belt.

2. When practicing in the Training Area:
   A. After you have finished in the dressing room, you will briefly review your last class, strike the bag, and apply stretching exercises while you wait for class to begin.
   B. Be dressed in proper uniform.
   C. Never chew gum.
   D. Never joke, laugh or talk excessively.
   E. Always try to keep your mind on the reason you are there.
   F. Absolutely no smoking on or near the area of training.
   G. Only on special occasions will food or beverages be allowed in the training area.
   H. Always be friendly and courteous to fellow members.
   I. Come to attention and bow when approaching or when approached by a senior member or Black Belt.
   J. It is respectful to address a senior member or Black Belt as "Sir" or "Ma'am" when speaking or when spoken to.

3. Appearance:
   A. The instructor or ranking student will make inspection of the student body to insure cleanliness and safety precautions.
   B. Personal hygiene is a must. Fingernails and toenails must be kept short and clean.
   C. One should always train in TaeKwonDo remembering the four simple rules of "true cleanliness":
      1. Clean Heart – Speak wrong of no one.
      2. Clean Mind – Think no evil thoughts.
      3. Clean Spirit – Be sincere in all your actions.
      4. Clean Body – Practice good personal hygiene.

D. Hair ruling for Men:
   1. Keep hair neat, clean and well groomed. Head bands and ponytails are optional but not recommended. Gentlemen with long hair are requested to tie their hair in a tight bun, ponytail or braid, thereby keeping it out of the way of practicing.
   2. Unless the student is growing a beard or mustache the student is expected to come to a formal class clean shaven.
E. Hair ruling for women.
   1. Keep hair neat, clean and pulled back away from eyes.
   2. Heavy steel hair clamps are not recommended.
F. Training Uniform (Toe'balk)
   1. Neat, clean and wrinkle free at all times when worn at class.
   2. All necessary patches and name sewn on according to regulations.
   3. Other equipment:
      a. All female students are required to wear a T-shirt under their toe'balk jacket. It is requested that the T-shirt be the same color as their belt.
      b. All male students are requested to wear athletic supporter with cup.
      c. Regulation arm and shin guards may be worn while sparring.
      d. School approved head gear, hand gear, and foot gear is recommended and in most schools mandatory for safety reasons and insurance regulations.
      e. Mouthpiece are highly recommended for sparring.
      f. Chest protectors are used for certain types of tournament competitions.

CUSTOMS & COURTESIES

WITHIN THE TOE'CHONG (TAE KWON DO TRAINING AREA)

RESPECT: Showing respect to others on or off the training floor is part of being a student in TaeKwonDo. While training, one should show respect at **all** times including to one's opponents. One should never lose patience, it is a sign of weakness. Maintain self-control and self-confidence at all times. As a beginner you will have two enemies: the lack of self-confidence and discouragement – don't let either overcome you.

1. Showing respect towards your Instructor.
    A. At no time in the training area or at any TaeKwonDo function are you allowed to refer to your instructor by his first name. If he/she is a 4th, 5th, or 6th Degree, it would be proper to refer to him/her at official functions or in correspondence or documents as "Master" (last name).
    B. When the Instructor enters the training areas for the first time prior to opening a class session, it is respectful to call the class to attention and bow.
    C. When an Instructor enters the training area who ranks below the rank of the Instructor conducting the class, no attention need be given.
    D. If an Instructor enters the training area that is above the rank of the Instructor conducting the class, it is proper protocol to bring it to the attention of the person teaching the class so that he/she may follow proper courtesy.
    E. When approaching or approached by your Instructor it is respectful that you come to attention and bow and always begin or end your conversation with "Sir or Ma'am."

2. Showing respect to what your training uniform represents:
    A. Never let your belt touch the floor.
    B. Always carry your uniform properly folded or inside a sports bag.
    C. It is now the choice of the Instructor if a student should remove his/her belt when doing something other than practicing TaeKwonDo. So, unless otherwise told to do so by your Instructor, leave your belt on at all times when in uniform.
    D. Never wash your Belt.
    E. Never wear the TKD uniform outside the training area unless you are practicing TaeKwonDo or are a part of an authorized public demonstration.
    F. While in uniform, a student must only practice techniques related to the training and teachings of TaeKwonDo, nothing else, unless approved by the Instructor.
    G. While seated on the floor, students should keep proper posture. There are only three positions in which a student may be seated on the floor. To learn them properly, the student must ask a Senior student to demonstrate all three.

3. When at a competitive event:
   A. Students are to gather at a site designated by the ranking Instructor, and it is at that point where "temporary headquarters" will be located. It is at this point where all valuables will be placed and secured by a responsible person. All awards and/or trophies are to be gathered at this location.
   B. When arriving or departing, it is requested that you first report to the "temporary headquarters."
   C. When awarded a trophy or medal, it is respectful to present your award to the Association President who then passes it to your Instructor who then secures it until the end of the event. In the absence of the President, you may award your trophy/medal to your Instructor. Have no fear, your trophy/medal will be returned at your request or at the completion of the tournament.
   D. Never voice your criticism of the event out loud or to strangers.

Master Ron Sell demonstrates a perfectly executed jump spin crescent kick.

PROFILE OF AN AMERICAN MASTER

2

FORWARD

I remember well the personal moments of private conversation with Master Edward Sell in the early years of my training. These moments became vehicles of pensive introspection for both of us. Moments when we spoke about unattached and unrelated subjects. It was like spinning a giant roulette wheel which was covered with thousands of occurences in each of our lives. When the wheel stopped, we were stimulated to discuss unhibitedly the subconscious word-picture which may have appeared.

The interesting phenomenon was the fact that no matter what the subject, it always evolved into a relationship with the martial arts.

He spoke to me one night late after a long and arduous day of instructing, about his earliest recollections of involvement in the field of self defense.

He began, "As a fifteen year old I found a Red Shouldered Hawk which had been abandoned by its mother. Although I was far from being an expert in the raising of this type of predator, I felt that destiny had lead me to the challenge, for the lessons it would teach me. I raised this magnificent bird to be a fine hunter and a self sustaining creature. We were inseperable for two years. One day some sixth sense told me it was time to release my friend back to its natural habitat and its predetermined way of life. As I released it back into the wild, it was as though I was releasing a part of my being. I found I needed an outlet for my bruised emotions. At that time I was accidently exposed to something called juijitsu. It seemed like an interesting outlet for a "touchy emotional condition." I pursued the study and practice of this form of martial art and mixed in some boxing, but no matter how hard I worked out, I always had the feeling that the real key to self defense was eluding me.

When I joined the Air Force and my orders carried me to Korea, it appeared to be just a duty stint. My exposure to the major styles of Korean Karate soon changed that attitude.

My assigned specific duty was in the Air Police, and ultimately evolved into self defense instructor for the Air Police.

I investigated the various styles of TaeKwonDo in the area surrounding Seoul, and after much soul searching I was convinced the broadest style was Chung Do Kwan.

I was fortunate in being able to study under some of the finest TaeKwonDo Masters.

When I returned to the United States I was sure I felt like the hawk I had trained and released! I personally have experienced the same emotions many times in training many Black Belts who were floundering in life's arena, and I gave them strong wings, and the necessary confidence through Chung Do Kwan to face life's challenges.

It is extremely fulfilling and gratifying to be blessed with the tools to aid these people in their development. I am still the falconer."

He is indeed the falconer! I personally have seen him work absolute miracles with students that, in some cases, had been turned away by other styles of the martial arts. Many of these students had emotional and physical handicaps that they required unremitting patience and compassion to cultivate them and nurture them through total commitment. Master Sell perservered, and was and is highly successful in the areas of physical emotional rehabilitation of thousands of aspiring students. He has been one of the outstanding American interpreters in the Korean language of the martial arts.

Robert G. Smith -- student & friend of Master E.B. Sell

WHAT IS A MASTER?

A Master is a person who has mastered the practical aspects of Taekwondo. In the United States Chung Do Kwan Association, all 4th Degree Black Belts are immediately eligible for the Associate Masters Degree. If they wish to master the art of teaching, they must continue the process of being upgraded in the Master Instructors Degree System. The training period at this level may be as much as fifteen to twenty years, depending upon the consistency, teaching abilities of the individual, personal growth and contribution to the goals and vision of the United States Chung Do Kwan Assoc.

- A Master has learned how to conquer any obstacle that would hinder him from developing as a whole person, in mind, body, or spirit.
- A Master must also have organizational skills in order to be a leader.
- A Master should be a role model who practices good morals by setting an example through his lifestyle.
- A Master is sensitive to the needs of others and practices the principles of the three F's when dealing with relationships, by being:
    (1) Firm-Standing for what he believes in, therefore gaining respect.
    (2) Fair-Showing compassion by listening to the needs and suggestions of others.
    (3) Friendly-Keeping the lines of communication open.

A Grandmaster is a teacher of Masters. The Kwan'Jang is a Senior Grandmaster, equivalent to the Head Dean of a college.

In 1968, Grandmaster Sell created and documented his Instructor Degree program. This system allows those Black Belts who wish to pass their knowledge on to others to progress not only in Black Belt rank, but also in elevated teaching skill levels. The USCDK Instructors Degree Program has allowed tremendous growth in this national association because of the incentives that have kept the retention of the Black Belt students who has the wish to become an Instructor. The following titles are earned independently of the rank with specific requirements and prerequisites to achieve them.

MASTER DEGREES

Master	4th Degree
Master Instructor	5th Degree
Sr. Master	6th Degree
Professor	7th Degree
Grandmaster	8th Degree
Sr. Grandmaster	9th Degree

THE KWAN'JANG
(THE MASTER OF MASTERS)

What is a Kwan'Jang? In Taekwondo terms Kwan means school, Jang means Director, Head Master, or Head Dean. Our school, or Kwan, is US Chung Do Kwan which I developed and organized in 1967.

To explain the various evolutionary stages of this ancient Korean martial art, I wish to take you back in time during my early years as a student Black Belt. I was serving my last two years of my second enlistment in the U.S.A.F. at Osan, Air Force Base, in Pyong Teak Kun, Korea when the political structure of Taekwondo began to change. In 1965, I was a member of the Tae Soo Do Chung Do Kwan Association, training for a 4th Degree Black Belt. I found this school (Kwan a particular system of training) to be a strong and very disciplined martial art, which was the reason it appealed to me. I soon discovered that there were at least sixteen different training systems of Taekwondo being taught throughout various parts of Korea at that time. Each school was called a "Kwan" (pronounced "Kwon"). The largest and most common that I can remember were Chung Do Kwan (my school's system), Ji Do Kwan, Sang Do Kwan, Moo Duk Kwan, Chang Moo Kwan, and Kang Duk Kwan. The founder or surviving Grandmaster of each of these schools were called the "Kwan'Jang." Each Kwan'Jang was looked at with the highest esteem.

After many rumors and false starts to form a unity among all the Kwans, the Korean Government decided to assist the many different Taekwondo schools with finances and special administrative assistance that would give Taekwondo national and international recognition. I can remember the pros and cons felt among many of the leading Korean Master Instructors about the government's support. At this time the word "Taekwondo" was accepted as the official name of this ancient Korean martial art. Problems began when the Korean Government decided only to recognize five Kwans: Chung Do, Ji Do, Moo Duk, Chang Moo, Kang Duk. This caused a split in many of the schools. It also caused hard feelings, jealousy and animosity within the ranks of the Masters and Instructors. The problems and poor attitudes began to reach new heights when the order came down that all Instructors had to be "re-certified."

In 1967, the president of South Korea declared Taekwondo as a national sport. For several years, the transformation of Taekwondo into an international martial art went relatively smooth with each Office of the Kwan'Jang governing it's own school and handling all the internal problems. Taekwondo was also introduced to the world as an "international sport" with the production and outstanding organization of the "1st World Taekwondo Championship" held in the newly built "Kukkiwon" building in Seoul, Korea. It placed Taekwondo among the elite sports of the world and I was extremely proud to participate in it as a Team Coach of one of three American teams that entered. I was also present when each of the participating countries approved the organization of the World Taekwondo Federation (WTF) and voted Dr. Un Young Kim as President. I felt that such actions were indeed historic events for the art, science and sport of Taekwondo.

When I was awarded the position of Kwan'Jang, I thought I had to be legalistic and tough. I really felt that the higher the martial arts position was, the more distant I should be from those under my authority. There is an old saying, "familiarity breeds contempt." Through the years I've discovered that is not true! God gives us wisdom as we look to Him. I realize now that people flock to excitement, but stay where they are loved. The life of a Kwan'Jang should be simple. He should teach others by example emphasizing that strength comes through humility.

Love is a word that has been very abused and distorted in our modern day society. Love is really an attitude that we develop that is as genuinely concerned about the welfare of others as much as we are ourselves. Love requires commitment and discipline, two of the key principles of Taekwondo. People flock to excitement, but stay where they are loved. Taekwondo is not abusive and neither should it's role models or leaders be abusive. We should be role models that cause others to search for the development of the spirit man, making us a whole person as explained on in Chapter 10 of this textbook. However, we can not be into ourselves, nor so heavenly minded that would prevent us from being down to earth to touch peoples lives. Respect is something you earn, not something you demand.

It is now my perspective that the position as an American Kwan'Jang should be carried by a person who has been consistently loyal, dedicated, experienced in Taekwondo and has exercised wisdom in his leadership abilities through Godly counsel. He is a man who has studied and trained in one system of teaching principles within the structure of Taekwondo for more than 20 years and been loyal to only one Kwan (school) all his life and confronts and successfully battles evil principles that continue to threaten the well-being of mankind. The Kwan'Jang desires to lead others to peace by creating harmony within the ranks of black belts and instructors; he is an arbitrator when needed. He strives to teach by example that strength comes through humility. Perhaps the most modern day translations for the position of Kwan'Jang would be the Head Dean of a university.

A true master is a servant. He doesn't demand respect, he earns it. He tries to touch peoples lives in a way that will help them to overcome the limitations that they themselves or others have put on them. He knows that a person needs to be strong in mind, body and spirit. I remember three distinct students who have taught me these valuable lessons. The following are only a few examples of the many experienced that I have been faced with:

A sixteen year old boy walked into my office with his father one cold winter day. His father sat next to him and began to tell me about his rotten, no good for nothing son. He said "the only thing my son wants to do is martial arts, so here he is, let's see what you can do with him." He had quit school and his father had basically thrown him out in the street. The boy had extremely low self-esteem and a stuttering problem. When he wasn't stuttering, he was mumbling. He was the kind of young man that carried a chip on his shoulder and was labeled a bully. I saw something in him, and took him on as a personal challenge. He was hungry for someone to love him, to care about him. I took him under my wing. He made black belt in 4 years. His life changed as he began to realize that his attitude determined his future, not his environment. He began to have a desire to change, and to swallow his pride in search of something better than what he had. One day, he came to me and said, "Grandmaster Sell, I've come a long way, but something is missing. Can you tell me what it is?" I handed him a Bible and told him to read the book of Proverbs to find wisdom. He carried his Bible in a brown paper bag with him wherever he went. He began to grow spiritually as he searched for wisdom. Today, he is married with a beautiful family, and an officer in the U.S. Air Force.

A young oriental man approached me at church one Sunday and asked if he could come by my office and talk with me. He came the next day. He was adopted by an American military family and raised in Germany. He felt rejected by all races and had just lost his sister to suicide. He was ready to give up. We sat and talked for several hours. Soon he began to train at my school. He finally found acceptance. He trained hard. Very few people thought he would make it. Many people became very critical about his mannerisms. I knew that deep inside him there was a key to unlock all of the hurt and rejection he felt. I not only trained him but I encouraged him to become a "whole man" (see Chapter 10). I began to watched him as he developed strength in his mind, body, and spirit. He became a new person. Today, he is married to a wonderful lady, owns his own Taekwondo school and is one of my most dedicated students.

Two young brothers walked into my office wanting to learn Taekwondo. They were green belts in a Japanese system and had just moved to Florida. They had rented a room together and were both suicidal. I took them in as students in an attempt to help them to discover that their life had a purpose. Through our Sell Team Ministry, my wife and I give crusades in prisons. I asked these two brothers to go with us. When I gave an opportunity for those who wanted a change in their life and to come forward and let me pray for them, they were the first ones to ask for prayer. Many prisoners followed them. When we returned home, they began to grow spiritually too. One moved away, and the other stayed. The one who stayed had at one time been on drugs, divorced with a small child, and had suffered with epilepsy. I began to treat him with respect and love, using the three F's talked about on page 33. Soon, he began to respond and I took him under my wing as a personal challenge to help him. Today he is married to a beautiful lady, who also became one of our Black Belt Instructors, has 5 children, earned his GED, completed trade school, teaches Taekwondo to underprivileged kids, and is a youth minister at his church. He found that the key to a balanced and stable life is to be a whole man; strong in mind, body, and spirit.

A good leader never gives up on a person, even when everyone else does. In these three cases, many people considered these people losers. There have been hundreds of stories such as these and many of my experiences with my students have touched my life in a very special way making me a better person and a better leader.

It is my desire to encourage all martial arts leaders, whether they be an Instructor, Master, Grandmaster or Kwan'Jang to learn the lesson that I did, "It is very difficult to touch and change peoples' lives perched high above them!" We must meet them at their level in order to influence them in a positive way. After all, isn't that what life is all about, leaving a positive impact that will motivate people towards becoming a better person and to be all that God wants them to be?

1967. The Beginning of a National Association:

While in Korea, Master Sell competed in many national tournaments and received much recognition and many awards never before given an American. He was a third degree Black Belt when he entered the 1963 TaeKwonDo Presidential Championship in Seoul, Korea, composed of three hundred competitors, 299 Korean Black Belts and one American, Staff Sergeant Edward B. Sell. Sgt. Sell represented both the USAF and the United States, and he was chosen as captain of his team by his fellow team members from Pyong'teak Kun, one of eight states in South Korea. It was the first time in the history of TaeKwonDo that a non-Korean was allowed to enter this annual event. The photo above shows Sgt. Sell sparring the Champion of Korea. Sgt. Sell did not win the match but he cherishes an honorable third place in that National event. A lot has happened in the life of Master Sell since that memorial event.

In 1967 Mr. Edward B. Sell created the Korean Tae Kwon Do Association of America (in 1975 changed its name The United States Chung Do Kwan Association) consisting of the teachings and principles of ChungDoKwan, one of the strongest and largest Tae Kwon Do institutes in Korea. With all the knowledge that he received at the many schools the United States Air Force has sent him to, including the USAF Judo Academy, USAF Leadership and N.C.O. Academies, plus many martial arts schools throughout Korea and Japan, Master Instructor Edward B. Sell combined his great wealth of knowledge acquired during his previous ChungDoKwan training, and added his own original ideas creating a training system he felt would develop and maintain the enthusiasm of the American Tae Kwon Do student.

Today, Grand Master Edward B. Sell is President (also called "Kwan Jang"), of his own association. The U.S. Chung Do Kwan Association is one of America's most uniquely organized institutes. Master Sell demands strict discipline from all schools within his association and the highest caliber of instruction from the many Black Belt instructors. "Unity in Uniformity" is the motto of his annual Instructor's Course that *all* Brown Belt and Black Belt students must attend.

Master Sell feels that he and his certified staff of Instructors can reach deep inside a student's soul and pull the very best of him out, thereby giving a student the confidence and pride to accomplish things that he normally would have never done.

Training at Osan Air Base, Pyong-Teak-Kun, Korea, 1962.

As a 1st Degree Black Belt, he was jumping as high as 8 feet, striking with a Flying Side Kick. His opponent in this picture was 6'6".

As a Green Belt, 6th Gup, Master Sell trained hard between classes. Here he practices the Flying Side Kick, (one of his favorite techniques).

1963. Grand Master Uoon Kyu Uhm congratulates Master Sell after he successfully tested for the 2nd Degree Black Belt with only 14 months training - the shortest time in history for an American.

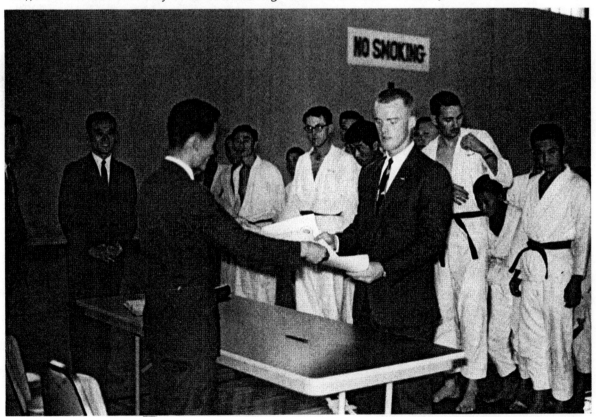

Upon Master Sell's return to Korea he reorganized his Instructor's School and built it into one of the most significant schools in Korea. For his efforts and dedication, the Grand Master awarded him a certificate of merit.

MUGGERS GET SURPRISED

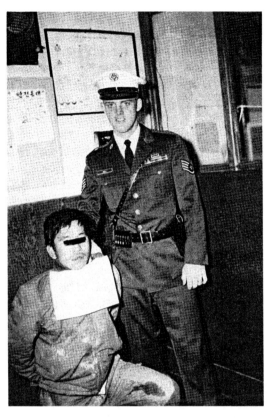

It's no secret that every country has a group of individuals that try to take advantage of others by cheating them, lying to them, or by stealing from them. Except for visitors lost in certain areas of our own large cities, the American GI in a foreign country is probably more vulnerable to these "human predators" than anyone else.

While stationed in Korea at Osan Air Base, 35 miles south of Seoul City, I spent most of my off duty time training at the Osan TaeKwonDo Club, which was sponsored by my unit, the 6314th Air Police Squadron. The rest of my time was spent trying to stay out of trouble and there was a lot of that available outside the main gates of our base. After my first nine months at Osan, I was promoted to a 3rd Gup Brown Belt. My instructors at that time were Mr. Myong Kil Kim and Mr. Tae Sung Yi, both 3rd Degree Black Belts.

It was early spring of 1962 when my commander, Major Hanson, came to our club and in so many words "volunteered" me to be in charge of what he called a "Decoy Squad" that was going to find the gangsters that had been mugging the GIs as they staggered back to the base after a wild night on the town. Up to that date, ten airmen had been badly beaten and all valuable possessions were taken from them. Six were hospitalized with brain concussions after being kicked in the head, which made the U.S. Base authorities think that it was a gang of renegade karate men. Since my commander volunteered me, it was my job to find out exactly who was doing this. Being a freshly promoted Brown Belt and having never given a thought to using my skills on another in actual combat, I was not sure if I wanted the job, although it soon became quite obvious that I had no choice in the matter.

After appointing two other fellow members to my "Decoy Squad," we were relieved of normal duties and began to make a plan to trap the gang that had been mugging our fellow airmen. During this period, the base curfew was still in effect, meaning that all American servicemen had to be back on base before 11 p.m. each night. There was one main gate, the only access point to get onto the base. It was within a dark alley a couple hundred yards from the main gate where most of the airmen had been jumped and beaten. The investigation revealed the existence of an informer in the base Airmen's Club who would watch the airmen to see who had large amounts of money and showed signs of intoxication. When a potential victim was spotted, the informer would alert the gang members outside the base gate. This meant that my squad and I had to do exactly that; flash money around and act as if we were smashing drunk. We had to talk about going down to the "V," better known at that time as "Chico Village."

After serving eight long years in the USAF, I have come to realize that this assignment was by far the most difficult one that I had ever had. Here I was in the Airmen's Club on payday night, trying to act like a complete fool which was totally against my code of ethics, and making believe I was getting drunk on a glass of icewater with a lemon and cherry inside it. My partner, Rich, had no problem, since he has been known to act like a drunken idiot without ever having had a drop of booze. At about 9:00 p.m. we started telling everyone that we were on our way to the "V" to spend all our money. Naturally faking it, arm in arm, we soberly "staggered" out into the street and hailed a taxi. The night air was cold and rainy as it had been for the past month. This was our second week at playing drunk and going down in the Village with no results. I figured that the gang should be getting hard up for money by then, and we both thought that, if it was ever to happen, this night would be the night. We visited three or four nightclubs, talked loudly, and made a few scenes in the street while we waited for the herd of GIs to head back towards the main gate making sure that we would be the last of the group.

There were two main footpaths (alleys) that all the homeward bound GIs took each evening. I sent my partner, Rich, to the alley least suspected to be the right one. As we split up, we both knew in our bones that I was going to be the target of that evening's mugging since I had flashed the most money around (most of which I had borrowed from my NCOIC Sergeant). The rain turned into a light drizzle as I headed towards the two big flood lights that overlooked the main gate.

Taking all the back alleys, I had about a quarter mile to go when I saw several silhouettes ahead of me that split up in two directions just past two rice barns on either side of the four foot wide path. I realized that I was the last of the pack and that there was no one behind me, making me a super target. I took my rain coat off, rolled it up, and placed it down on the ground about fifty feet before stepping out from between the two barns. I took no more than two steps, when a little Korean kid came out of nowhere and ripped off my new regulation type USAF rain coat. He was gone in a flash. After giving him only a glance, I realized that I was not acting very drunk. So I started singing some dumb, off-beat tune as I began to approach the last heavily shadowed area leading to the main gate. With each step my heart beat harder and faster. I could almost taste the adrenalin racing through my body. I quickly took my cap off and placed it in my back pocket and checked the button on the pocket containing my money and the money borrowed from my sergeant.

As soon as I cleared the opening I turned sharply to my right, high blocking a punch directed at my face. In the same instant, I felt a sharp pain, a ripping sensation down my back. It was later determined that a can opener had ripped my shirt and caused a long gash down my back. My mind became blank but I felt myself react to every move made by my assailants. I side-kicked the person that had attacked from behind, threw another over my shoulder as he grabbed me from behind, front snap-kicked another very hard in the groin and round-kicked two more in the head. It was at this time that I realized there were four attackers actually fighting me. After dropping three of them, I threw the fourth on top of the other three and piled them in the corner. After knocking three unconscious and seriously hurting the fourth I turned in time to see the "ring leader" running down a very narrow path between two rice patties. I chased him for about fifty yards, then hit him in the side with a flying side-kick which almost planted him is a rice paddy. In fact, I had to reach down and grab him by the hair and pull him out of the muck, otherwise he would have drowned. I dragged him back to the others, most of whom lay very still, took out two pairs of handcuffs and began to secure legs and arms in the muddy pile of bodies. Trying to catch my breath and realizing that all this actually had happened, I turned around, sat down on top of them to make sure that no one left the scene and I began to blow the whistle that each of us carried to alert both the Air Police and KNP (Korea National Police). It was at this time I started to make an immediate inspection to see if I was in one piece. Other than a ruined uniform, one shoe missing and a scratch down my back, I seemed in good shape. I looked down at my muddy watch and realized that the whole encounter took less than two minutes, which included dragging the "boss" to the scene where it all began.

In conclusion, the Base Commander bought me a new uniform, my Commander bought me a new raincoat, my Sergeant bought me a new pair of shoes, and the next promotion that came around had me receiving a new stripe. The muggers were properly convicted and Osan Air Base never heard of airmen being mugged by Koren gangsters again. None of these men had any formal training in TaeKwonDo. If they had, they would not have been found in the position. From that day on, I became a true believer in Taekwondo as an art of self-defense and the power that the human body can deliver when properly trained.

I found some humor in this story in 1965, after a one year leave from Korea. I was re-stationed at Osan Air Base and I decided to have dinner at Osan's NCO (Non-Commissioned Officer's) Club. I began talking to a few of the sergeants who told me the story of the red headed Air Policeman that single handedly whipped twenty five Korean gangsters, killing ten of them using Taekwondo. I grinned, walked away and had my dinner.

"TAE KWON DO INTEGRITY AND INGENUITY COMBINE TO MEET A TROUBLESOME CHALLENGE"

This incident happened sometime between my Green and Brown Belt training at Osan Air Base, Pyon Teak Kun, Korea.

It was a hot summer day and most of the guys in my unit, including myself, received three-day passes. Rather than go to the local Village or to the big city of Seoul, I contacted one of my Instructors and made arrangements with him to train all during the Fourth of July weekend. I was hoping to "double test" from 5th Gup (Class) Green Belt to 3rd Gup Brown Belt. Therefore, I felt that I needed all the training and practicing I could get, especially after hearing that very few Americans had ever successfully double tested from 5th Gup.

We all know that every school, job, classroom, and military unit has "big-mouth bullies," who think that they know everything and try to control everything and everyone smaller or weaker than themselves. My Air Police Squadron was no exception. His name was Billy Williams, and he called himself "Wild Bill" (naturally). As usual, he had a pack of followers that were not any nicer or didn't know any more than he did, which wasn't anything much. He stood 6 foot 7 inches and was the star on the base football team. He weighed about 250 pounds and spent a lot of time lifting weights. He and I didn't get along from the start, especially since he had this thing against martial arts and made fun of TaeKwonDo whenever he had the opportunity. I was pleased that he was never assigned directly to the same unit that I worked with.

One day, I was on my way to an evening TaeKwonDo class when he and his "Wild Bill gang" stopped me and actually challenged me to fight. I never believed he would really attempt to do something so dumb. I gave some serious thought to ignoring him and walking right on by, but he insisted and wanted me to show exactly how effective TaeKwonDo was. He began to rattle-off at the mouth and called me many names along with the insults. Then he actually began to push me, at which time I had the right to strike back, but I didn't. I tried my best to ignore him.

At this time my Instructor and a handful of fellow students stood outside the door of our Toe'chong (school) and watched to see what my next move would be. I told him that I had no intention of fighting him, because that was not the purpose of my training. However, if he was serious about challenging me, I would fight him after demonstrating the power of TaeKwonDo. Remembering that he and many others were always asking me to break a board or brick to show the effectiveness of TaeKwonDo, I told him to find the biggest board he could find and bring it back to me in one hour. If I couldn't break it, I would fight him. After realizing what I had said, I wasn't exactly sure what my next move would be. I've been in many situations throughout my life where I "played it by ear", and I guess this was no exception. I went to my class as usual and was coached by my Instructor and fellow students.

About an hour later, Wild Bill and his followers showed up outside the Chung Do Kwan Club where I had trained twice daily ever since my arrival in Korea. He brought the biggest piece of wood that any two men could carry. Actually, it was a piece of "railroad tie" about 10" x 10" x 4'. I expected him to do exactly that. No way could I, or even King Kong, break that slab of wood. I looked at my instructor as he looked at me with raised eyebrows, which meant, "it is time to test your skills," but I was not going to accept that. I saw that it took two men to carry the block of wood, so, I began to make the arrangements to break it. I told Wild Bill that I needed at least six more people to hold the piece of wood while I jumped through the air and kicked it with the edge of my foot. He didn't hesitate to volunteer six of his followers to grab a hold of that log and lift it shoulder high in preparation for the dramatic break (which would definitely have made the Guiness Book of Records "plus"). All during the time that the board holders were properly stationing themselves, locking out on the elbows and back legs and all the other technical preparations needed to make a break that "Superman would be proud of", I was

Edward B. Sell
Korea, 1973

wishing that I was some place other than where I was. Then, out of the clear blue sky, it came to me.

I decided to ask Wild Bill himself to stand and help hold the board at the "center position". He cheerfully accepted and stationed himself directly behind the 10-inch thick piece of wood. I began a series of leg stretching exercises, a few push-ups, and then positioned myself about twenty-five feet in front of the board holders. By this time we had aroused the curiosity of many other GI's around the area, including a few that had cameras. I personally suggested a few choice spots for those who wanted to take pictures, then assumed a fighting stance. I let out a loud yell, took several running steps, jumped in the air and flew directly over the piece of log that everyone was holding and hit Wild Bill right between the eyes with the edge of my foot, knocking him unconscious to the ground. Recovering from the five-foot leap, watching everyone else pick themselves up from the staggering impact of one of TaeKwonDo's most powerful kicks (a jump or flying side-kick), I asked "Would someone else please hold this board while I try again'?" There were no volunteers, and most important, there was no fight.

Wild Bill recovered in a short time with a mild headache, and became a true believer in TaeKwonDo.

Airman Bill Williams and I became good friends, and even though he only had a short time left in Korea, he spent many hours at our TaeKwonDo Club and became a 5th Gup Green Belt before leaving Korea.

Designed By: Edward B. Sell – 1967.
The emblem inside the circle was designed by Master Sell from one of his own photos. The name of his studio was "The Academy."

"A YOUNG BLACK BELT AMAZES HIMSELF WITH THE POWER OF CHUNG DO KWAN"

This story takes place on a Southern California Military Installation where I was assigned as an Air Policeman. I had just returned from my first duty in Korea. I was a very young, ambitious 2nd Degree Black Belt trying to learn all that I could about the Oriental Martial Arts. I was very disappointed to find that there were very few good quality Karate schools in America at this time, and none near my Air Force Base. So I practiced alone at the base gym every day, keeping myself in shape and reviewing all that I had learned during my first 14 month tour at Osan Air Base, Korea. Outside of eating, sleeping and doing my Air Force duties, I did nothing but practice TaeKwonDo.

In my younger days as a teenager, long before I became interested in the Martial Arts, I enjoyed hunting. Each year I could hardly wait for the Michigan Small Game season to open, followed by deer season in mid-November. I considered myself to be a darn good hunter and sportsman. I always tried my best to make a clean kill so that the animal did not suffer. If I did wound an animal, I never gave up until I found it and made sure that the meat would not go to waste. I became upset when I saw other hunters shoot their game and waste the meat, or make no attempt to find an animal that they had wounded.

I not only hunted animals, but I studied them. As a boy I enjoyed raising young orphaned animals: raccoons, oppossums, squirrels, crows and even a fox. My main hobby was Falconry. It took me five years, but I actually trained a Red-Shouldered Hawk to hunt from my wrist. That species of hawk is by far the most stubborn and hardest to train bird in the world. I loved nature and learned about animals through my own experience with them and the many books that I read about them. At one point in my life I seriously thought of becoming a veterinarian or a game warden, to help and protect the wild animals.

Well, let me get back to my story. On this Air Force Base there was a serious problem with the deer population. The Base was very large and fenced in, and for many years, there was no hunting allowed in the isolated areas outside the main operation center and residential areas of the Military Installation. Consequently, the deer were beginning to cause automobile accidents on the winding, mountainous roads. Also, the deer herds were becoming a serious threat to the large landing fields where some of the largest USAF aircraft were in operation. It seemed that on cool evenings the deer would lay on the runways, which had absorbed the heat of the day, making it very dangerous for the aircraft to take off and land. The Base was right on the coast; and during certain times of the year, the nights would become unusually cold when the breeze shifted off the Pacific Ocean. At that time of the year as many as 100 to 200 deer would lay out on the runways.

Naturally, the Base Commander was having a fit over this problem and it was rumored that the deer would be poisoned and left to rot. The local authorities and conservationists protested this inhumane method of solving the problem. The next best solution was to have an "Open Season" on the deer and assign only the best marksmen, since the deer herds were congregating in areas where a stray bullet would damage aircraft and fuel depots. Only classified personnel were chosen because most of the Base was classified as Top Secret and civilian personnel were not allowed access.

My Air Police Squadron was assigned to this job. All the meat was to be processed properly and distributed to all the under-privileged families in the local area. Personally, I felt that all the men picked to be hunters for that period did a good, neat job, with no incidents of suffering on the part of the animals that were to be "thinned out." It was a job that had to be done in order to save human lives and to prevent a disaster on the runways.

It was the last day of the hunt when my unbelievable story takes place. My partner Jim Bruno and I were assigned to a section of land southwest of the Main Operations. It took in a long strip of beach area that was well-known for having all night swimming parties. We had already gotten six deer that afternoon. It was about 6:00 p.m. and we began to head back to the APO (Air Police Operations), knowing that we would probably be up all night processing the day's deer kill. As we came near a sharp curve in the road, a big deer jumped out in front of us nearly causing our truck to go off the steep cliff which would have put us on the beach below. Jim had not had much luck that day and he wanted a last chance to bring down his second deer of the day. The deer stopped about a hundred yards to our left. Slowly, Jim took his rifle (USAF 30 Cal. Carbine), opened the truck door, and positioned himself to shoot. Just as Jim fired, the deer got spooked, which brought the alignment of the bullet back from the shoulder about a foot, meaning that the animal was "gut-shot." "Wow!" I thought to myself, "All day we had clean shots, not one deer was wounded, and now we are on our way home, it's getting dark, and we've got to track down this deer which could run for miles and miles before finally dying." Neither one of us felt very good about it. We must have tracked that deer five miles in a complete circle before the evening darkness set in. It was now about 9:00 p.m. We began driving up and down all the back roads hoping to find this wounded animal. Fortunately, it was all open area, with no trees, only short bushes which would make it difficult for a deer that size to hide. The trail looked as if the deer was heading down toward the beach with aviation (jet fuel) gasoline storage tanks directly in the background. This meant trouble, because if the beach and fuel tanks were in the background, we couldn't shoot it without risking the possibility of hitting a night-time swimmer or rupturing one of the large fuel storage tanks.

Using the truck's spotlights, we were straining our eyes, scanning across the fields and sandy areas. Finally we saw a bright set of eyes. At first it looked as if the deer was laying down and then stood up as we shined him. He was directly between us and the fuel storage area and a portion of the beach. Therefore, any chance of using a rifle was eliminated. There was but one chance, and that was to blind him with the spotlight, sneak up behind him and hit him in the head, hoping that it would do the job and we could end this nightmare. Jim thought that I was joking, until he saw me take off my boots and begin crawling through the sand to the far left. The deer stood petrified, while Jim held the light directly in its eye. Barefoot, as I was slowly angling myself behind the animal, I realized that I did not bring anything to strike with. The distance from the truck to the deer was about 75 yards, but I was beginning to feel that I was crawling for a mile or more, moving very slowly. Finally, I was directly behind the deer; getting to my feet, I slowly stepped closer and closer, knowing that I was going to have to hit this hard-headed animal with my hand. Immediately, the thought of Master Mas Oyama, who has killed bulls with his bare hands, flashed through my mind. I told myself, "Hey, this isn't funny. This is a serious position that I have placed myself in and it is my obligation to put this wounded animal out of its misery." With that as my last thought, I cocked my arm back and slammed the edge of my hand behind the ears of this young buck. The animal leaped straight into air, kicking my cap off my head with his back hoof, nearly removing my nose, and then dropped to the ground and was dead instantly. I began to tremble after realizing exactly what I had done. It seemed like a dream, but it was very real. I saw the spotlight go out as Jim ran over to see what had happened. It was difficult for him to believe that I hit the deer with my bare hand. The deer had two six-inch "spike horns" sticking up from his head. It didn't take me long to realize that if he had only turned his head one inch, I would have pierced my hand with his antler.

It was late and we had worked a long shift. We loaded the deer into the truck and drove to the freezer lockers where all meat coming onto the base was stored. The Air Police commander had assigned "non-hunter" air policemen to the midnight shift and it was their job to field-dress the deer during the night and await the arrival of the Base Veterinarian to inspect the carcass in the morning. (In the modern Air Force each base is assigned a veterinarian whose duties are not the traditional "animal care;" his job is to inspect all foods coming onto the base for the dining halls, and he also serves as the public health officer for the base.

Just as "reveille" was about to sound over the loudspeakers the next morning, I was awakened by a runner from Base Operations with the word that I was to get myself over to the freezer lockers on the double. Quickly dressing, I jogged double-time across the base to find the vet, the Air Police commander and the headquarters commander all engaged in some kind of "conference" over the carcass of my "karate-chop" deer. "What is this, Sell?" my captain demanded (he was from Wichita Falls, Texas and was a very good deer hunter himself). "This critter doesn't have a single bullet wound in its body!" The base vet was puzzled. He had the carcass up on a table and was doing a full-dress autopsy on it. "Look, Sell," the captain said, "Uncle Sam doesn't authorize you to play around with karate on official duty time. I want to get to the bottom of this." With that we hopped in the AP jeep and drove back to the scene at the fuel storage tanks. We found the spot where Jim's "gut shot" had hit the animal and, now in daylight, it was easy to follow the blood trail. About a hundred yards into the brush we found Jim's animal, gut-shot and all, lying dead at a spot that I calculated to be about 20 yards from the spot that my karate chop ended the life of his brother! Fantastic you say? Remember, this place was just crawling with hundreds of deer; it is a feat that any other Black Belt with a deer-hunting background could have accomplished with that many deer around!

TaeKwonDo Times

WORLDWIDE COVERAGE

MARTIAL ARTS, FITNESS AND HEALTH

SEPT. 1988
$2.50
CANADA $2.95

EDWARD SELL
Is He America's First Master?

JEAN FRENETTE
Forms Superstar Stunts His Way To Film Success

BONG SOOL
Developed in The U.S. Our Own Martial Art

GETTING OUT OF JOINT LOCKS
The Other Side Of Hapkido

TRADITION OF NO TRADITION
Combines Korean Martial Arts And Kickboxing

THE SWORD CANE
007 Techniques That Bond Your Enemy

ALCOHOL AND THE MARTIAL ARTIST
A Lethal Marriage Of Destruction

NEW CONTEST
WINNERS EVERY ISSUE
(See Inside)

THE WHOLE MAN

" To become strong in mind, body and spirit."

As President of the United States Chung Do Kwan Association and Author of this textbook. I cannot and will not compromise my belief in God. I base the philosophical aspects of my entire TaeKwonDo training and career upon the foundation of the Christian faith.

I have felt a special closeness to God throughout my entire life, especially during the ages of 6 through 10 which I consider to have been the critical years of my youth. My mother divorced my father and it was during those years I turned to God for the "fatherly image" that a young boy needs at that time in his life.

Actually, it was at the age of three that I experienced my first miracle, one of many that have been continually happening in my life. I accidentally fell on a sharp knife and stabbed myself in the left eye. The doctors thought that I would be blind but my parents and grandparents prayed asking God to heal my eye. The wound took twenty six stitches and the scar is still visible today. After several weeks, the doctors removed the bandage and patch that I wore over the eye and to their amazement, the eye was completely restored.

I went to Sunday school during my elementary years and began to learn more and more about God and His Son, Jesus Christ.

When I was 10 years old, my mother remarried. My new Dad was nice to my younger brother and me and he had a great concern about our spiritual growth and made arrangements for us to attend a Christian school. It was during these years that the things of God really began to make sense to me. I actually found my place with God when I realized the truth of what the New Testament of the Bible is all about. But like most young boys and teen-agers, I did not apply the teachings to my life. I had the "head knowledge" but I did not allow it to fall into my heart until much later in my life.

Then came the second miracle. Due to a foolish and reckless accident, I was shot in the side with a .22 caliber rifle. The bullet went through my spleen, grazed my lung, missed my heart by a fraction of an inch, broke a back rib and spun around in my stomach a few times. I actually thought that I was going to die. Knowing God, I prayed "Dear God, don't let me die!" God answered my prayer and even though there was a serious operation and over one hundred stitches and much internal repairs made, He healed and delivered me from this close brush with death. As I was recovering from this accident, I entertained the thought of becoming a Christian minister. The fact that I was one of four brothers and a sister, kind of stifled the reality of that dream, at least I thought so at the time.

Thanks to my hard working parents, my teenage years were happy ones. I had plenty of opportunity to become involved in a wild and reckless life but God installed a special alarm system in my heart. Everyone has one but not everyone can hear it. I believe He made mine extra loud because of the future plan that He had in store for me. That alarm system is called "a conscience". It went off whenever I felt myself step out of the boundaries that my parents and my Christian faith instilled in me. I must admit that there were a few times when I didn't hear it because the carnal man in me didn't want to hear it. But thank God, most of the time I avoided trouble when I saw it headed my way. That is one of the key principles of my teachings to young people: "Avoid people, places and things that cause trouble."

GRANDMASTER E. B. Sell's Personal Testimony

At the age of seventeen, a senior in High School, I decided to go all out for football. Due to my gunshot wound, I was unable to participate in sports since it took over four years for it to completely heal. It was hard work, but I made the team, "first string half back Varsity Squad". Wow! I was excited about the possibility of getting a school letter and finally making my mark in a sport. The night before the first game, I woke up with terrible pains throughout my body and an extremely high fever. My family and I didn't realize it at the time, but I was actually dying of an acute ruptured appendix. The poison had already begun spreading throughout my body. Normally a person would die within a 30 minute period after that happens. I didn't want to go to the hospital so my mother doctored me through the night, but the pains became worse the following morning. I prayed for God to take charge of the situation and He did. I was rushed to the hospital but all tests showed negative., Exploratory surgery was suggested; that's when they make an incision on your body and hope it is the right place. God lead them to the problem, because the doctors were baffled, telling my parents to pray, not giving much hope. To their amazement they removed a ruptured appendix the size of a grapefruit. Another ninety stitches and six weeks later God completely healed me, but I never played that football game.

After graduating from High School, I decided to join the U.S. Air Force. Due to a weak self-discipline, I had a tough time adjusting to the military way of life. However, by asking God to give me the strength each night, I made it through. It was during this time of my life that I began hearing many war stories about the martial arts. I read every book that I could get my hands on. Judo was the most popular at the time and the limited exposure that I received during Air Police (military police in the USAF) training only put fuel on the fire of my excitement to learn more.

After becoming permanently stationed at Selfridge AFB, Michigan, I volunteered for duty to the Orient, specifically to train in some kind of martial art. There were no commercial schools like we now see available in most cities. No one at that time even dared to make a profession out of teaching Judo or Karate.

Finally after a long waiting period, I received orders for duty at Osan Air Force Base, Pyong Teak Kun, Korea. Once there, I immediately began training. I went through instructors like most people go through old newspapers. I wore them out, I couldn't get enough. At that time the martial art that I was training in was called Tae Soo Do Chung Do Kwan, to me it was Korean Karate, and I loved it! I became the first person in history ever to be tested for a 2nd Degree Black Belt in a record of eleven months total training. Today, I believe that the Korean Masters that approved the special examination actually expected me to fail but I didn't. I wish to interject that I now believe that everything that I experienced up to this time period of my life, was indeed in God's Master Plan for me. Performing in front of the top Masters of the world and passing that 2nd Degree Black Belt examination within such a short period of time was another one of God's miracles and the beginning of my international fame that catapulted me into the upper ranks of TaeKwonDo.

My relationship with God was as strong as I thought that it should be. Little did I know that even though I was not the righteous Christian that I should have been, He still cared enough to set the path for me to follow. I actually thought that my soul was saved and that if I died, I would certainly have a place in heaven. I look back at that time today, and I would not want to bet on it. I thought that all I had to do was believe and be as good as I could. I know now that even "Satan believes" and that "no one gets to heaven by good works". If I would have died and gone to heaven, it would be by the skin of my teeth. I also know now that my life would have been a lot easier and I would have received many more of God's blessings if only I had known then what I know now. I believed in Jesus Christ but I did not allow him to take control of my life. I resisted the opportunity to become totally committed to the life style that is expected of a Christian, a "Christ-like person."

The national reputation that I created throughout Korea caused my instructor to ask me to remain in Korea for another tour of duty so that I could become the highest ranked American ever in the art and science of TaeKwonDo. The thought of such a title stimulated my ego. Unfortunately, my first four year enlistment was up and I had to return to the U.S. for discharge. I explained to my instructor that I would return to Korea somehow, even if it meant re-enlistment in the Air Force. Somehow, I knew that I would be back in a short time. God and I had many sincere discussions about all the possibilities. You see, God wants us to talk to Him just as we would talk to our natural father. He wants to know every thought and be a part of everthing that we do, regardless of how simple it may seem. Even though I may not have gotten a "gold star" for my behavior at times, I made it a point to be on bended knees each and every night, no matter how many bumps and bruises I received during my extensive training. There are many times in our lives that our spirit becomes bumped, bruised and even broken, but knowing that we can **ALWAYS** turn to God in prayer is what keeps the spirit of man alive and constantly seeking after God's will.

Due to my stubbornness and unwillingness to yield to the Call of God in my life, a fourth brush with tragedy was in the making. I used to believe that God caused all the hurt and tragedies in one's life, but since becoming a "Born Again Christian", I now believe that man causes all his own hurt, pain and tragedies by refusing to listen to the calling of God in his life. I have read in the Bible where Satan is named as "the Prince of this world" and he will take advantage of anyone who is not within the protective graces of God. The next experience in my life became miracle number four, and I find it difficult for me to tell at times because it is hard for people to believe it. But it was in God's plan for me to have this almost unbelievable testimony that would be the beginning point of my own Christian ministry.

It was in the Spring of 1964, I had just returned from Korea, extremely excited about my new 2nd Degree Black Belt. A few friends and I were having a good time diving off a bridge near my home on a river in Rockwood, Michigan (a suburb of Detroit). We were diving head first from 18 feet into 12-1/2 feet of water. The next day my friends called me up and invited me to go back down to the bridge. When I arrived, they "dared" me to dive off head first. Here is where a case of "peer pressure" nearly took my life. God does not want us to become victims of peer pressure. He wants us all to be successful and reach our full potential. If we try to impress people and be like other people, we are not being "ourselves" thus we are totally out of character with what God has planned for us. He wants us to "be all we can be" not be like someone else. This type of attitude and accepting the challenges of peer pressure can cause serious consequences, injury and even death. Remember the " Alarm System" I talked about earlier? We must learn to listen for it and take the warning seriously. For some reason, perhaps because of my ego, I didn't hear the alarm when it went off. I dove head first without checking to see that the tide had gone out and the river had dropped eight feet. I am now diving into 4-1/2 feet of water. I hit the bottom so hard that I saw two bright lights in my eyes, and a piercing sound in my ears. I know now that I was near death because I felt a peace surround me, but I also heard a strange voice in my mind telling me to "Inhale! Inhale!" It was obviously the voice of Satan trying to take my life. Satan speaks to us through our mind and God talks to us through our hearts and spirit. The problem that most people have is that they listen to their own mind more often than they listen to their heart. The heart of man is his spirit and it is his spirit that puts man close to God and it is the spirit of man that God uses to communicate with man. I am thankful for my Christian upbringing, and for the spirit that God has created in me, I listened to my heart and allowed God to take over my entire being at that moment. I felt peace and warmth all over my body. From the center of the river there was a distance of at least 60 feet. My friends panicked. I don't remember swimming to shore. When I finally became conscious, I was lying on a hospital bed with a strange strap attached to my chin and a cable attached to the strap that went under my bed with a large weight attached to the cable. I then realized that I was in traction. I then began to feel the terrible pain and frightening look upon the faces of family and friends leaning over my bed. I remember the doctor telling me that I will never walk again because I have a broken neck! After hearing those words it was as if a shock wave was sent through my body. I just could not accept it, but I was reminded of it when I tried to lift my arms and found myself paralyzed from the shoulders down. I cried out to God and said, "God! Where are you? This can't happen to me!" For days my mother would come in and feed me. She would also pick pebbles out of my head that were imbedded from hitting the bottom so hard. All that my carnal man said and did during that time of helplessness I cannot remember, but I do know that my spirit man was continuously in direct communication with God who gave me the peace that the Bible talks about so often.

In my spirit man I prayed, "Oh Heavenly Father, thou are the creator of the universe and the Almighty Physician. There is nothing that is imposible for you. You know all my thoughts and deeds. You know what my life-time ambition is. I ask that you get me up out of this bed and help me accomplish the goal of becoming the highest ranked Black Belt any American ever received and I promise that I will search out the plan that you have for me and I will serve you and some day tell boys and girls, men and women about the miraculous power of prayer and that it does work and that there is a living God called Jesus Christ."

Within ten days after I said that prayer, I walked out of that hospital. The doctors gave me one of those white collars that looks like it should be around a horses neck. They said that I would have to wear it for four years. I lost it in three days. They also said that I would never pass the physical examination for re-enlistment in the Air Force and that I would never be able to practice TaeKwonDo again nor would I be able to move my neck normally. Within thirty days from saying that prayer, I was back in the U.S. Air Force. Within sixty days after I said that prayer I was back in Korea at the same Air Force Base training for my life-time goal.......Within twenty years after the accident, your's truly, Edward B. Sell, received a most coveted award within the TaeKwonDo Black Belt ranks, the Seventh Degree Black Belt never before awarded to anyone outside of the Korean Nationality; not just the highest ranked American, but an international record, the highest ranked "Non-Oriental in the World". Today, I am telling hundreds and thousands of people this story and giving my Lord and Savior, Jesus Christ the Glory for allowing me the privilege of forming a strong communication with my Heavenly Father.

My story could easily end there. But I have not allowed it to end, as a matter of fact it is just beginning, because God has shown me a source of power and a peace of mind that passes all human understanding that I wish to share with you. About five years prior to officially being notified of the 7th Degree promotion, God created a stirring in my heart that took me out of one of my largest TaeKwonDo businesses into a warmer climate (The Bible Belt of Florida) where I have attended Bible College and churches that have really excited the spirit man in me so much that it has become "Born-Again" just as Jesus talks about in the book of St. John, Chapter three. Recently, I accepted the Ordainment into the Christian ministry, and I am doing my best to live up to the promise that I made to God nearly twenty five years ago.

For more than twenty five years, I have shown hundreds and thousands of my students how to become strong in two critical areas of life, "in body through the physical training of TaeKwonDo and in mind through practice and training of self-discipline and learning how to concentrate by ridding the mind of all outside problems." Many of my students became leaders and Black Belts, but after a period of time they began sliding backwards into the same old routine and life-style which was followed by similar problems and weaknesses that they had in the past. I did not realize it then as I do now, that in order to become a "**Whole Man**" and receive **all** the benefits that being a Whole Man has to offer, that one key ingredient was absent. That was the teachings on how to become spiritually strong, by getting to know the Almighty Creator.

If anything that you have read or I have said has touched you or stirred the spirit man within you, it was not me. It was not what I wrote, it is God calling you to seek after Him and find out what He has planned for you.

If you would like to know more about the spiritual strength that I have found, I suggest that you get God's Word and begin reading the Gospel of Jesus Christ (the first four books of the New Testament, Matthew, Mark, Luke and John). Then, start looking for a church that teaches the truth, exactly as you read in the Bible.

My prayer to you and all the students, parents and non-practitioners of the art is that the spirit man within you finds the peace, joy and happiness that God has intended for you.

Grand Master Uoon Kyu Uhm, President of the World Chung Do Kwan Association, awards Edward B. Sell one of many outstanding achievement awards while his instructor, Grand Master Hae Man Park stands to his left.

9th Degree Promotion of Edward B. Sell

Great Grandmaster Uoon Kyu Uhm, Vice President of the World Taekwondo Federation and President of the World Taekwondo Chung Do Kwan Association (WCDKA), Grandmaster Hae Man Park, Vice President of WCDKA award Grandmaster Sell his 9th Degree Black Belt dated August 10, 1997. Photo taken in the Kukkiwon at the office of World Taekwondo Vice President Uoon Kyu Uhm. Professor Brenda is to his left.

Grandmaster Sell and Professor Brenda at the Kukkiwon, World Headquarters November, 1997.

In the Kukkiwon, Grandmaster Sell points to himself in a historic photo of the committee present during the formation of the World Taekwondo Federation.

Grandmaster Sell and Professor Brenda are honored guests at a Black Belt examination in Korea.

A celebration dinner in Korea in honor of Grandmaster Sell's new promotion to 9th Dan.

AUTHOR'S PHILOSOPHY ON THE TEACHING OF TAE KWON DO

When a child is born he lacks four important skills and principles of life needed to survive in today's American culture: coordination, discipline, self respect and defensive reflexes. All four must be taught to the child and, as he matures, he must develop strength in all areas of these principles.

If an infant is not taught how to walk properly, he will crawl on all fours or walk with a hunched back. Through coaching and practice, he is taught coordination & how to use his hands properly. As he grows, school sports pick up where his parents left off and he begins to polish his coordination and maximize the use of his talents.

As an infant, the human must be spanked or scolded for doing wrong so that he remembers. All through life he must learn to accept the consequences for doing wrong and must learn from his mistakes. A weak person reflects a weak discipline. As he matures, the punishment for doing wrong becomes more severe, strengthening his self discipline so that he does not continue to make the same mistake, and preventing him from doing anything more serious.

Through parental guidance, the child is taught self respect and respect for others. Without this principle, he will not be popular among friends or accepted in society and may develop criminal tendencies. With proper guidance, he will learn all about personal hygiene and take pride in his appearance and accomplishments, which are the foundation in the building of a strong, self-confident individual.

No one is born with the knowledge of self defense. It is something that all of us hope that we will never have to use. However, with the crime rate increasing everyday, you can be sure that it is on the minds of everyone. Everyday we read in the newspaper of the rapes, muggings, and killings throughout the nation and in the local area in which we live. To learn how to defend yourself properly with your bare hands and feet can be looked upon as being a kind of "insurance." TaeKwonDo Korean Karate is in fact the simplest form of self defense for anyone of any age to learn, and by far one of the worlds most perfected systems of fighting.

While training in the art and science of TaeKwonDo one can find fulfillment of all these four principles of life.

"Professor Brenda" demonstrates a controlled side kick to her son "Master Ron."

SIX PARTS OF A TAE KWON DO CLASS

3

SIX IMPORTANT PARTS OF A FORMAL TAE KWON DO CLASS SESSION

1. **STRETCHING EXERCISES**
   (Student loosening up 10 to 15 minutes prior to class)

2. **BASIC FUNDAMENTALS**
   (At the command of the Instructor)

3. **FORMS, also known as Poom'se/Kata**
   (Patterns of movement to strengthen defensive reflexes)

4. **ONE-STEP SPAR**
   (Blocking and counterattacking a set, predetermined form of attack)

5. **FREE SPAR**
   (Simulated combative situation, striking and kicking without inflicting pain or injury to opponent.)

6. **FINISHING EXERCISES**
   (To assure that all muscles have been stimulated)

PART ONE
STRETCHING

Stretching is part of the warming-up exercises and perhaps one of the most important exercises in TaeKwonDo. By practicing a proper routine of stretching exercises, you will lessen the possibility of injuring muscle tissue as you learn to strike out harder and faster while increasing your skill.

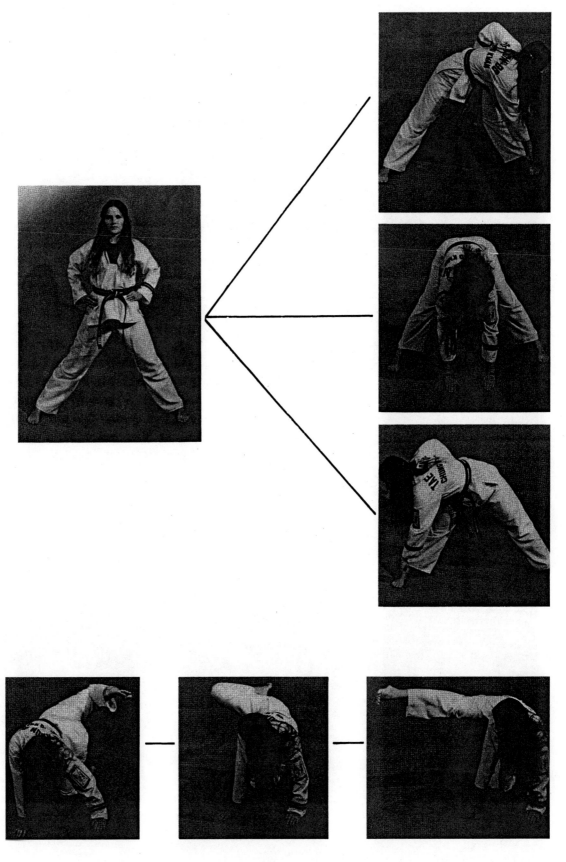

60

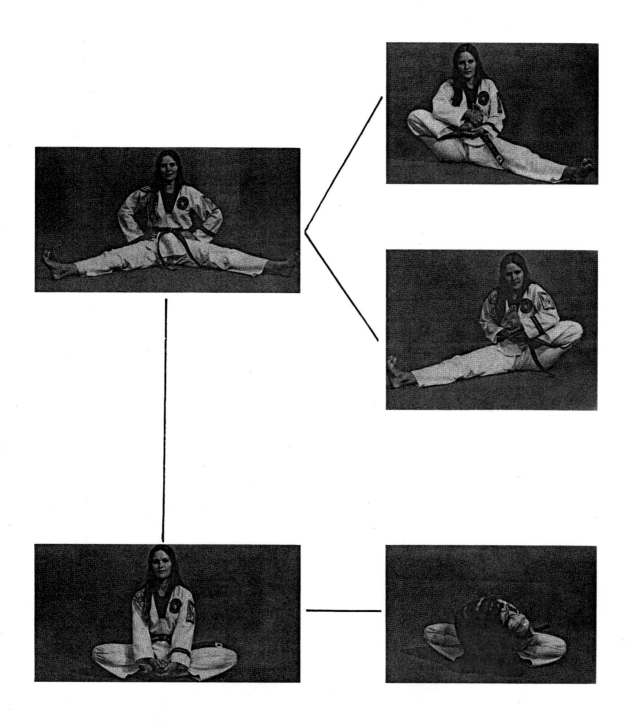

Practice these important exercises daily, if possible.

PART TWO

THE 15 BASIC FUNDAMENTALS

There are "Fifteen Basic Fundamentals" constantly practiced by all students, regardless of rank, at the beginning of each regular class session. These techniques may also be referred to as "warm-up exercises." The constant practice of these fundamentals keeps the students' muscles at the highest tone of conditioning. Each time the students execute these techniques they should try to put *more* power and precision into each move. *"Constant repetition is the pathway to perfection."*

CHIM'BEE (Ready)

FOREWARD SQUARE STANCE

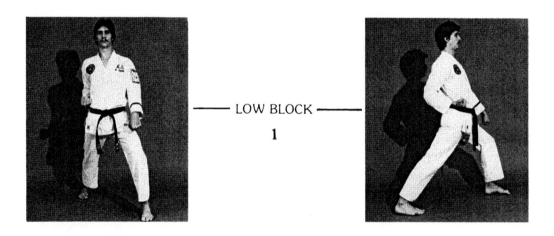

LOW BLOCK

1

 —— LOW PUNCH ——
2

  —— HIGH BLOCK ——
3

 —— HIGH PUNCH ——
4

Mid-Section Block - side view

MID-SECTION BLOCK

5

PREPARATORY POSITION (front-up)

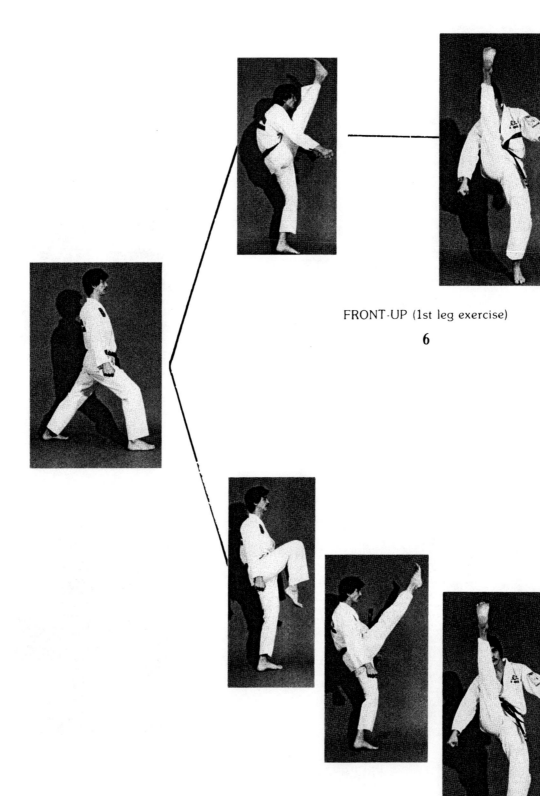

FRONT-UP (1st leg exercise)
6

FRONT KICK
7

––– SIDE-CHOP –––

(Body Weight 50/50)

8

"T" STANCE

FACE-CHOP

(Body Weight 80/20)

9

OUTSIDE BLOCK
(Body weight 50/50)
10

FIGHTING STANCE
(Body Weight 80/20)
11

Fighting Stance

The Round-Kick (also known as the Round-house-kick), when properly executed, can be the most powerful blow delivered by a human. In Chung Do Kwan, we use both the ball of the foot and the top of the foot as striking points: The ball of the foot when practicing Forms/Kata or when breaking boards; the top of the foot when sparring or while competing in tournaments, since it prevents serious injury and also adds three to four inches of length to the foot in order to score a point.

ROUND-KICK

12

(Front View)

Striking with the top of the foot.

Striking with the ball of the foot.

STRADDLE STANCE

The Side Up is not a technique, it is a leg exercise that conditions the student's legs so that he can execute the side kick properly without pulling or tearing muscle tissue. It is almost impossible for a man who has had no formal training to execute a side kick properly without causing injury to himself. He must first condition his legs.

SIDE-UP

13

SIDE-KICK

14

(Front View)

"T" Stance

Square Stance

15

The first combination technique called "Yuk'jin"

SIMPLE PRINCIPLE IN BODY BALANCE

A human arm varies in size and weight, but when it is thrown outward from the body due to the centrifugal force created as the body spins or moves forward, the weight of the arm is surprisingly increased. Therefore, if the arm is not held in tight, or centrally placed in the middle of the body, the extra weight of the arm will pull in the opposite direction from the body and cause the body to be unbalanced or unstable when recovering from a particular movement. By bending the arms at the elbow, (at a 30-45 degree angle), and bringing the arms close into the chest and solar plexus area, one has centralized the majority of the upper part of one's body weight and can maintain good body balance, allowing an easy recovery from a technical movement. This practice also creates a unique cover over the vulnerable torso areas which places the arms in the perfect position for blocking and counterattacking.

Additional Fundamentals

PIVOT SIDE-KICK
16

Pivot on Foreward Foot as Right Leg is cocked in.

Side-Kick

SPIN-KICK
17

Pivot Backwards on Left Foot as Right Leg is cocked in.

Side-Kick

Fighting Stance

REVERSE CRESCENT KICK
18

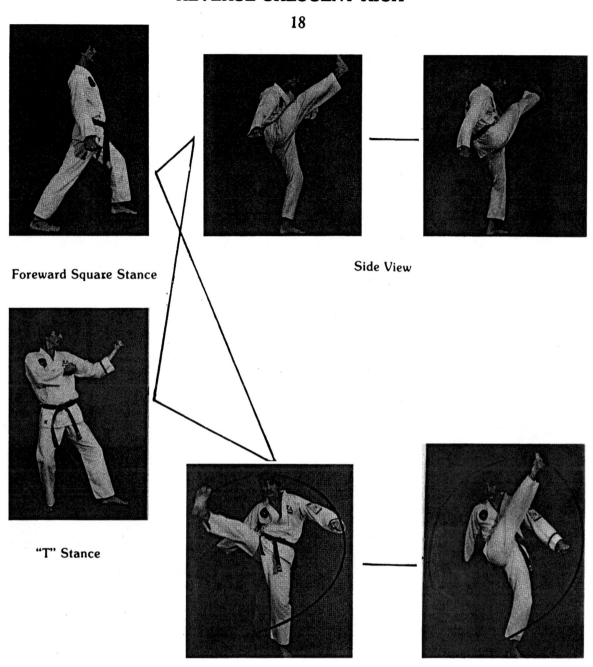

Foreward Square Stance

"T" Stance

Side View

Front View

Note: When applying either the inside or outside crescent kicks the circumference motion should be as wide as the student is tall. This indeed takes much practice.

CRESCENT KICK   CK
19

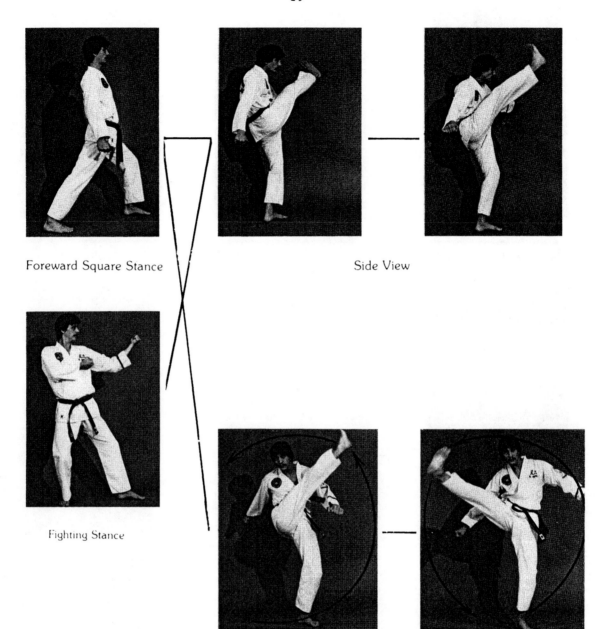

Foreward Square Stance

Side View

Fighting Stance

Front View

ADDITIONAL BASICS

PIVOT SLAP ROUND KICK
20

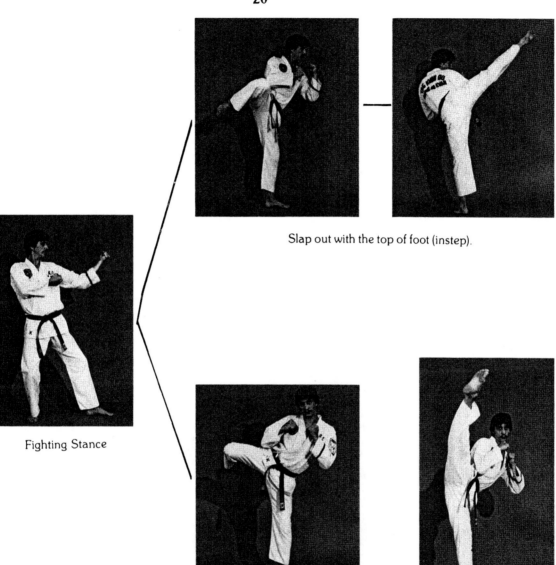

Slap out with the top of foot (instep).

Fighting Stance

Front View

This kick has made history in American tournament competition. It takes much practice to develop "knock-down" power with the shifting of body weight, otherwise it is only effective in scoring points or stunning an opponent. It also can be considered as one of the fastest kicks applied by a human.

75

The author refers to these kicks as "people movers." Both are very powerful, and can do a lot of damage if not properly controlled while sparring.

21
JUMP SIDE-KICK
(Flying Side-Kick)

Strike with foreward foot while in mid-air.

Jump off the foreward leg, cock both legs in.

Fighting Stance

22
SHUFFLE SIDE-KICK

Shuffle off both insteps, cock foreward leg in.

Strike with foreward foot as rear foot touches floor.

JUMP FRONT-SNAP KICK
23

Strike with foreward foot before touching floor with rear foot.

Jump off foreward leg as both legs are cocked in.

24
SHUFFLE FRONT-SNAP KICK

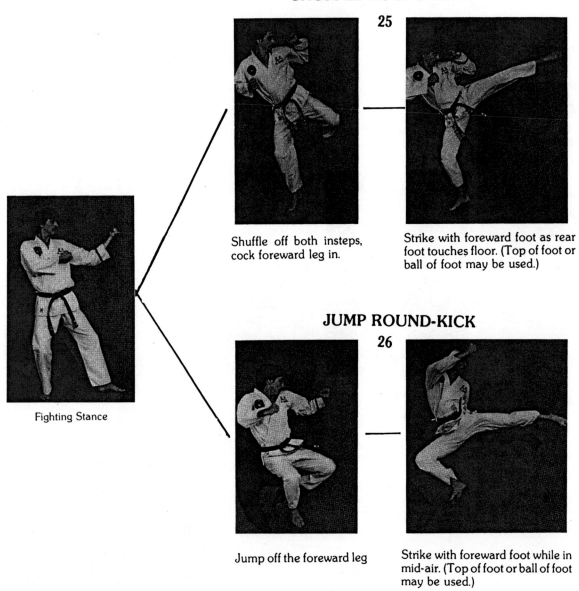

SHUFFLE ROUND-KICK
25

Shuffle off both insteps, cock foreward leg in.

Strike with foreward foot as rear foot touches floor. (Top of foot or ball of foot may be used.)

Fighting Stance

JUMP ROUND-KICK
26

Jump off the foreward leg

Strike with foreward foot while in mid-air. (Top of foot or ball of foot may be used.)

27
HOOK-KICK

Fighting Stance

Right foot crosses behind left foot.

Lift foreward off floor as high as possible; hook the lower part of leg, striking with heel or ball of foot.

28
PIVOT HOOK-KICK

Pivoting on foreward foot, swing rear leg foreward as if to front-snap kick.

Twist hips sharply and reach out with toes as lower part of rear leg is "hooked" backward.

SIX WAYS TO APPLY A KICK

In 1980, while reviewing my notes for an annual Instructors' seminar, I discovered an amazing secret that will revolutionize your training and/or teaching methods when applying the kicking techniques.

There are basically six distinctive ways of applying every kick.

1. STATIONARY KICK — Meaning that there is no linear movement; the kick is delivered from the foreward foot. (see Fig. A)

2. PIVOT KICK — Pivoting on the foreward foot, the kick is applied from the rear foot. (See Fig. B)

3. CROSS OVER KICK — Stepping over the front foot with the rear foot, the kick is delivered with the front foot. (See Fig. C)

4. SHUFFLE KICK — This kick is used to cover distance quickly. Using the strength of the insteps push off with the rear foot, shuffle foreward (also referred to as a Lunge) kicking with the foreward foot the instant that the rear foot touches the floor. (See Fig. D)

5. AERIAL KICKS

    A. JUMP KICK — This kick is used to gain height and can be applied from the stationary position or after two or more steps foreward; using the strength in the lower legs, jump and kick with the same foot in mid-air at the maximum height; recovering on the rear foot. (See Fig. E)

    B. FLYING KICK — After much training, this kick can be used for both height and distance; propelling one through the air from the strength in the upper and lower legs for maximum height plus foreward body momentum for distance. It is applied very similar to the Jump Kick, except more emphasis is placed upon speed to increase the foreward momentum of the entire body. (See Fig. F)

6. DROP KICK — Considered a more advanced kick not to be practiced by beginners or intermediates. This kick may be considered after all else has failed, in the case of self-defense situation. It is applied simply by dropping straight downward and excuting a kick straight upward, or it can be applied following a rollout maneuver. You will find a photo of this technique on page 211.

**After one has mastered these basic kicks, the student is then encouraged to combine the application. When the student is able to successfully apply the various combinations, he has then entered into the advanced stages of kicking techniques.

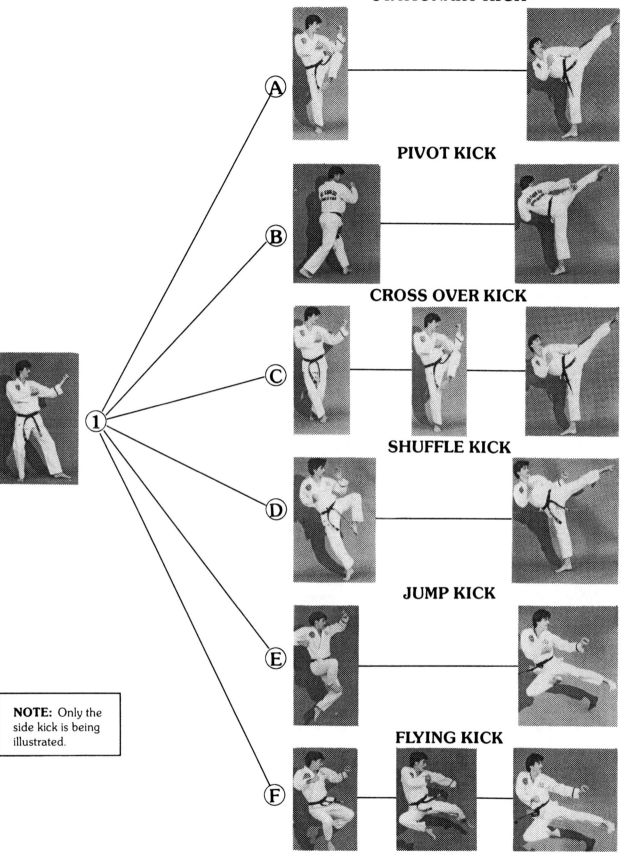

NOTE: Only the side kick is being illustrated.

83

PART THREE
POOMSE

Poomse is the continuous practice of exercise that is essential in the development of the fundamental qualities necessary for Taekwondo performance: body balance, accuracy, concentration, coordination and endurance. Thus, "without Poomse there is no Taekwondo". Throughout this manual we will refer to them as Poomse and Forms.

Forms are found in all styles of Karate. Forms can be described in many ways . . . "A specific pattern of defensive movements...An exercise or training method used when a student is able to imagine that he/she is being attacked by three or more persons, from three or more different directions, and uses the many tools of Taekwondo to defend himself against imaginary assailants...The beginning of the *computerization* of an individual's defensive reflexes...The uniting of several singular offensive and defensive moves into a dance-like form...The beauty and self-discipline of the art and its practitioner...A form of mental relaxation...A form of meditation...A test of one's memory...A physical and psychological exercise...A form of expression...A unique method of learning one's full use of arms and legs...A test of attitude and enthusiasm...etc....

The primary objective of Forms is to create and strengthen defensive reflexes. Forms also help a student develop a unique self training program. Most of the basic techniques are executed many times throughout the formal exercises, providing the student with an opportunity to review these techniques until he has perfected them.

A Poomse can consist of a pattern of movements ranging from sixteen basic moves to over two hundred advanced defensive techniques, depending on how skilled or proficient the student may be. The use of Poomse gives the advancing student an opportunity to use the **many** striking, kicking and punching techniques within a sequence of single and combination movements. This develops a unique system of defense within the student's reflexes and counter-attacking ability without having to take the time to "think out" each specific move when actually attacked by an assailant. Forms teaches a student to "focus" his train of thought and strengthen his self-discipline through intensive concentration.

The Author has classified these formal exercises into several categories: Beginner, Student; Advanced Student; and Black Belt Student. As the student is promoted through the various ranks, the Forms become more difficult and complex. At the writing of this book, a student must memorize 10 forms as perfectly as he possibly can before completing the series of requirements necessary to be promoted to the first level of the Black Belt ranks, called "1st Degree (Don or Dan)". At the time of being tested, the student is expected to perform his Poomse "exactly" as it was taught to him by his Instructor. Therefore, he is graded on basic techniques, physical fitness and enthusiasm, a system very similar to that used to grade a contestant in gymnastics or figure skating at Olympic events.

Practice each form with a clear mind and concentrate on every movement until the techniques become a part of you. This will reflect your interest and enthusiasm in the art. It is here that "Constant repetition is the pathway to perfection."

INTRODUCTION TO THE TAEGEUK POOMSE

The Taegeuk forms put into patterns of movement the foundation of techniques upon which TaeKwonDo is built. From the Taegeuk forms the student learns to develop overall coordination, power and body balance. This allows the student to develop an ever-increasing knowledge and ability in TaeKwonDo. Tae means bigness, Geuk signifies eternity; therefore, these forms should be practiced with an open mind and an increasing awareness. Each form has its own unique philosophy and characteristics.

As the student promotes through the ranks they find the forms progress from the hard, rigid techniques to a smooth flowing power. This should be in accordance with the student's own developing fluid motion, continuing to develop power yet with speed and ease of movement.

The Taegeuk forms are set in an 'H' pattern with a center cross bar which is to be performed on the way up or back down the middle of the form. These forms consist of three sets of three directions each, with each set of movements making use of blocking and/or counter attacking techniques to either side and the middle. With the exception of one form, the midsection punch is used exclusively in these forms.

The Taegeuk forms introduce a short or walking square stance. The inside block is used frequently and reverse techniques are found throughout these forms (the opposite arm is used from the leg that is forward).

Practice these forms diligently and enthusiastically and you will be well on your way to becoming a U.S. Chung Do Kwan Black Belt.

The Taegeuk Poomse are the official forms of the World Taekwondo Federation, Seoul, Korea.

TAEGEUK IL CHONG
(1)

Taegeuk One represents the ancient principle of Heaven and Light. This form teaches blocking low, middle and high as well as alternating between straight and reverse techniques. The short dominates this form with the long square stance used only up and down the middle of the form.

1. LOW BLOCK (L) (Left)
2. PUNCH (R) (Right)
3. LOW BLOCK (R)
4. PUNCH (L)
5.   A) LOW BLOCK (L)
    B) REVERSE PUNCH (L)
6. REVERSE INSIDE BLOCK (R)
7. REVERSE PUNCH (L)
8. REVERSE INSIDE BLOCK (L)
9. REVERSE PUNCH (R)
10.   A) LOW BLOCK (R)
    B) REVERSE PUNCH (R)
11. HIGH BLOCK (L)
12.   A) FRONT KICK (R)
    B) PUNCH (R)
13. HIGH BLOCK (R)
14.   A) FRONT KICK (L)
    B) PUNCH (L)
15. LOW BLOCK (L)
16. PUNCH (R) GIYUP

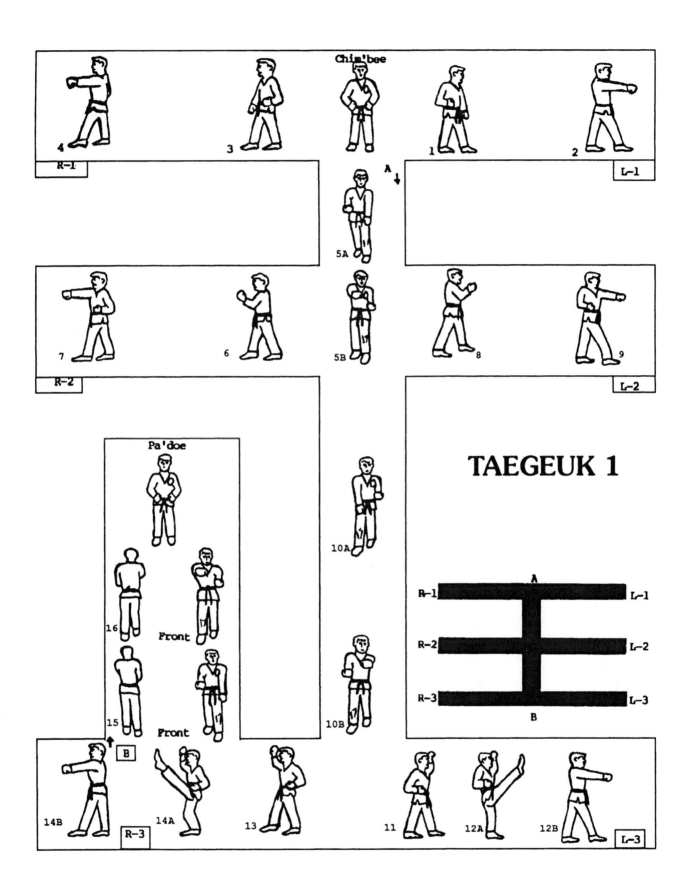

TAEGEUK Ee CHONG
(2)

Taegeuk Two represents the ancient concept of Joy. There are only two high punches found in the Taegeuk forms, these are in set two of Taegeuk Two. Short stances are once again used, and the only long square stances are found with punches that are to the sides of the form.

1. LOW BLOCK (L)
2. PUNCH (R)
3. LOW BLOCK (R)
4. PUNCH (L)
5. REVERSE INSIDE BLOCK (L)
6. REVERSE INSIDE BLOCK (R)
7. LOW BLOCK (L)
8. A) FRONT KICK (R)
   B) HIGH PUNCH (R)
9. LOW BLOCK (R)
10. A) FRONT KICK (L)
    B) HIGH PUNCH (L)
11. HIGH BLOCK (L)
12. HIGH BLOCK (R)
13. REVERSE INSIDE BLOCK (L)
14. REVERSE INSIDE BLOCK (R)
15. LOW BLOCK (L)
16. A) FRONT KICK (R)
    B) PUNCH (R)
17. A) FRONT KICK (L)
    B) PUNCH (L)
18. A) FRONT KICK (R)
    B) PUNCH (R)   GIYUP

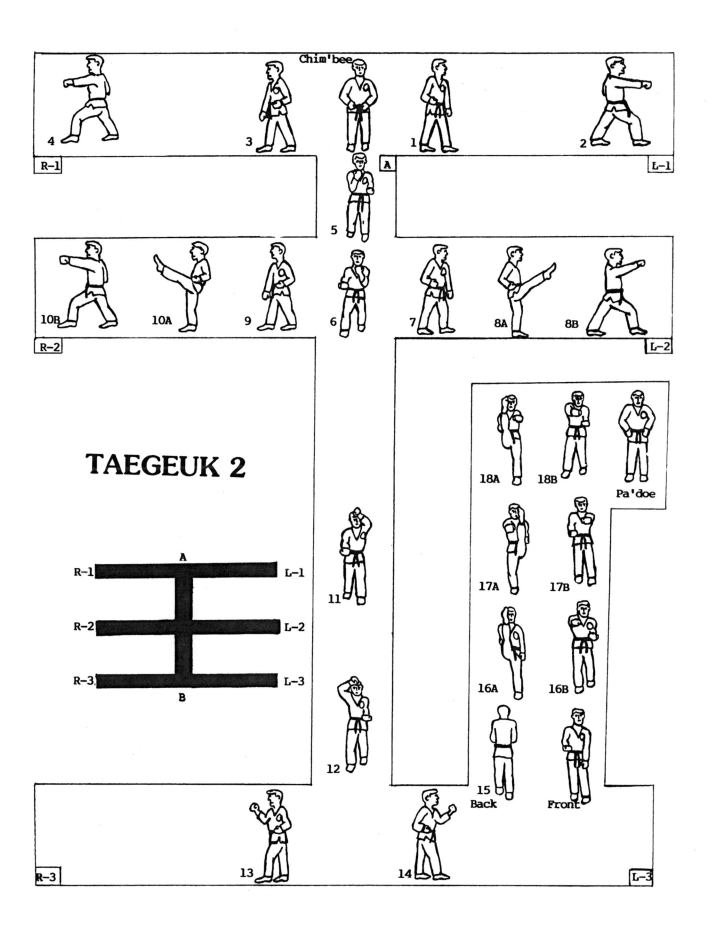

TAEGEUK SOM CHONG
(3)

Taegeuk Three, represents the ancient philosophy of fire and sun. This form introduces open-handed techniques as well as stressing combinations. Once again the long square stances are used only on punches to the side of the form.
(Note: The notation of L or R represents the foreword foot, remember a reverse technique is the opposite hand movement of the foreword foot.)

1. LOW BLOCK (L)

2. A) FRONT KICK (R)
   B) PUNCH (R)
   C) REVERSE PUNCH (R)

3. LOW BLOCK (R)

4. A) FRONT KICK (L)
   B) PUNCH (L)
   C) REVERSE PUNCH (L)

5. REVERSE INSIDE SUTO (L)

6. REVERSE INSIDE SUTO (R)

7. OUTSIDE SUTO BLOCK (L)

8. REVERSE PUNCH (L)

9. OUTSIDE SUTO BLOCK (R)

10. REVERSE PUNCH (R)

11. REVERSE INSIDE BLOCK (L)

12. REVERSE INSIDE BLOCK (R)

13. LOW BLOCK (L)

14. A) FRONT KICK (R)
    B) PUNCH (R)
    C) REVERSE PUNCH (R)

15. LOW BLOCK (R)

16. A) FRONT KICK (L)
    B) PUNCH (L)
    C) REVERSE PUNCH (L)

17. A) LOW BLOCK (L)
    B) REVERSE PUNCH (L)

18. A) LOW BLOCK (R)
    B) REVERSE PUNCH (R)

19. FRONT KICK (L), LOW BLOCK (L), REVERSE PUNCH (L)

20. FRONT KICK (R), LOW BLOCK (R), REVERSE PUNCH (R) Giyup! (yell)

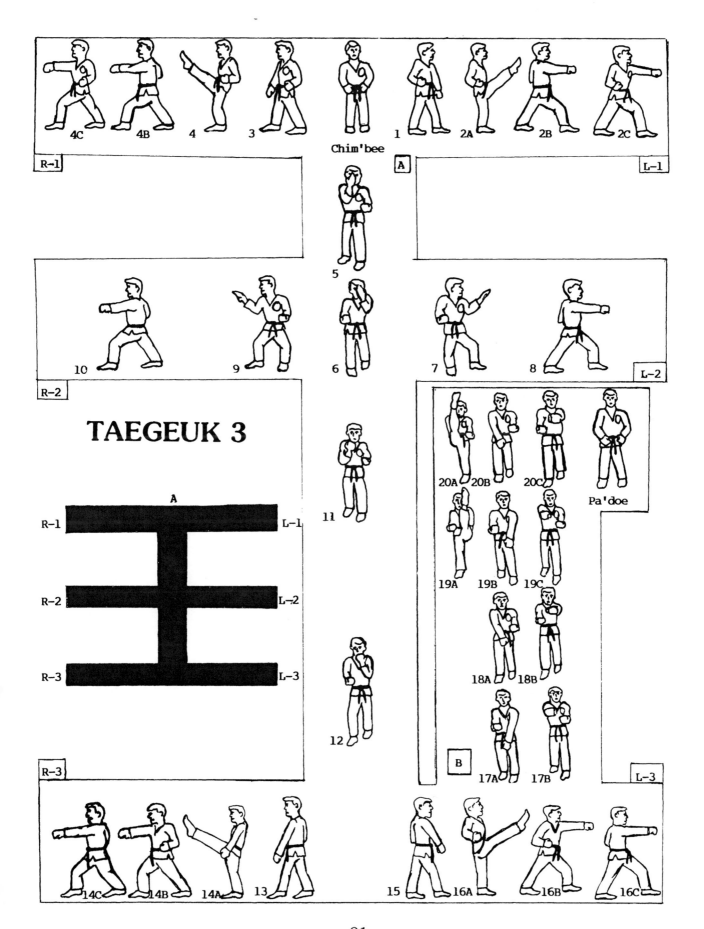

TAEGEUK 3

TAEGEUK SA CHONG
(4)

Taegeuk Four symbolizes the ancient philosophy of Thunder. This form breaks away from the rigid movement of the previous forms and is considered the first of the advanced poomse. The form makes use of a more fluid motion and introduces two-handed techniques as well as the hammer block. The short or walking stance is almost eliminated at this point with the exception being on the two stances to the sides of set three. In addition, Taegeuk Four uses a backwards sliding parrying movement.

1. FACE CHOP (L)
2. REVERSE CHECK BLOCK /SPEAR HAND (R)
3. FACE CHOP (R)
4. REVERSE CHECK BLOCK / SPEAR HAND (L)
5. HIGH SUTO BLOCK /REVERSE INSIDE SUTO (L)
6. A. FRONT KICK (R)
   B. REVERSE PUNCH
7. PIVOT SIDE KICK (L)
8. A) PIVOT SIDE KICK (R)
   B) FACE CHOP (R)
9. HAMMER BLOCK (L)
10. A) FRONT KICK (R) *Replace right foot and then,*
    B) *Slide forward foot back* REVERSE INSIDE BLOCK (L)
11. HAMMER BLOCK (R)
12. A) FRONT KICK (L) *Replace left foot and then,*
    B) *Slide forward foot back* REVERSE INSIDE BLOCK (R)
13. HIGH SUTO BLOCK (L) /REVERSE INSIDE SUTO (R)
14. A) FRONT KICK (R)
    B) BACK FIST
15. A) INSIDE BLOCK (L)
    B) REVERSE PUNCH
16. A) INSIDE BLOCK (R)
    B) REVERSE PUNCH
17. A) INSIDE BLOCK (L) ,B) REVERSE PUNCH   C) PUNCH
18. A) INSIDE BLOCK (R) ,B) REVERSE PUNCH ,C) PUNCH GIYUP!

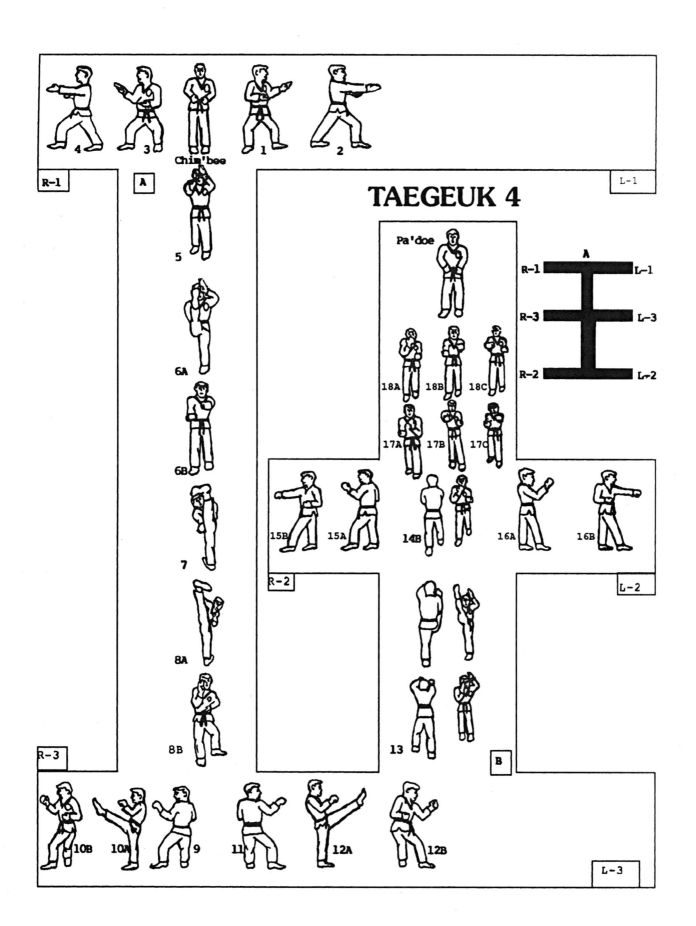

TAEGEUK OH CHONG
(5)

Taegeuk Five, the ancient philosophy of Wind, makes use of hand combinations which includes the hammer blow, back fist and elbow techniques. The square stances are all long stances.

1. LOW BLOCK (L)

2. *Slide forward foot back to L- Stance* Overhead HAMMER BLOW (L)

3. LOW BLOCK (R)

4. *Slide forward foot back to L- Stance* Overhead HAMMER BLOW (R)

5. A) INSIDE BLOCK (L)
   B) REVERSE INSIDE BLOCK

6. A) FRONT KICK (R)
   B) VERTICAL BACKFIST
   C) REVERSE INSIDE BLOCK

7. A) FRONT KICK (L)
   B) VERTICAL BACKFIST
   C) REVERSE INSIDE BLOCK

8. BACK FIST (R)

9. OUTSIDE SUTO BLOCK (L)

10. ELBOW STRIKE (R) *Fist into palm*

11. OUTSIDE SUTO BLOCK (R)

12. ELBOW STRIKE (L) *Fist into palm*

13. A) LOW BLOCK (L)
    B) REVERSE INSIDE BLOCK

14. A) FRONT KICK (R)
    B) LOW BLOCK
    C) REVERSE INSIDE BLOCK

15. HIGH BLOCK (L)

16. A) PIVOT SIDE KICK (R)
    B) REVERSE ELBOW STRIKE *INTO PALM*

17. HIGH BLOCK (R)

18. A) PIVOT SIDE KICK (L)
    B) REVERSE ELBOW STRIKE *INTO PALM*

19. A) LOW BLOCK (L)
    B) REVERSE INSIDE BLOCK

20. A) FRONT KICK (R)
    B) BACKFIST WITH STOMP (R) **GIYUP!** *Slide left foot to Twisted or Cross-legged Stance.*

TAEGEUK YUK CHONG

Taegeuk Six, symbolizing the ancient philosophy of Water, once again uses a backwards parrying motion. The smooth flowing circular techniques represent the yielding yet powerful motion of water. The palm block is first used in this form.

1. LOW BLOCK (L)

2. A) FRONT KICK (R)

   B) Replace kicking foot-Slide forward foot back-OUTSIDE HAMMER BLOCK (L)

3. LOW BLOCK (R)

4. A) FRONT KICK (L)

   B) Replace kicking foot-Slide forward foot back-OUTSIDE HAMMER BLOCK (R)

5. REVERSE CIRCULAR SUTO BLOCK (L) Shoulders Twisted to Left

6. ROUND KICK (R) Set foot down and step out with left foot

7. A) HAMMER BLOCK (L)

   B) REVERSE PUNCH (L)

8. A) FRONTKICK (R)

   B) REVERSE PUNCH (R)

9. A) HAMMERBLOCK (R)

   B) REVERSE PUNCH (R)

10. A) FRONT KICK (L)

    B) REVERSE PUNCH (L)

11. DOUBLE LOW BLOCK (L) Left foot moves to Chimmbee position -Slow Semi-Tension

12. REVERSE CIRCULAR SUTO BLOCK (R) Shoulders twisted

13. ROUND KICK (L) GIYUP Set foot down and spin into

14. LOW BLOCK (R)

15. A) FRONT KICK (L)

    B) Replace kicking foot-Slide forward foot back-OUTSIDE HAMMER BLOCK (R)

16. LOW BLOCK (L)

17. A) FRONT KICK (R)

    B) Replace kicking foot-slide forward foot back OUTSIDE HAMMER BLOCK (L)

18. Right foot steps back toward middle-FACE CHOP (L)

19. Stepback-FACE CHOP (R)

20. A) Step back-PALM BLOCK (L)

    B) REVERSE PUNCH (L)

21. A) Step back-PALM BLOCK (R)

    B) REVERSE PUNCH (R)

    GIYUP

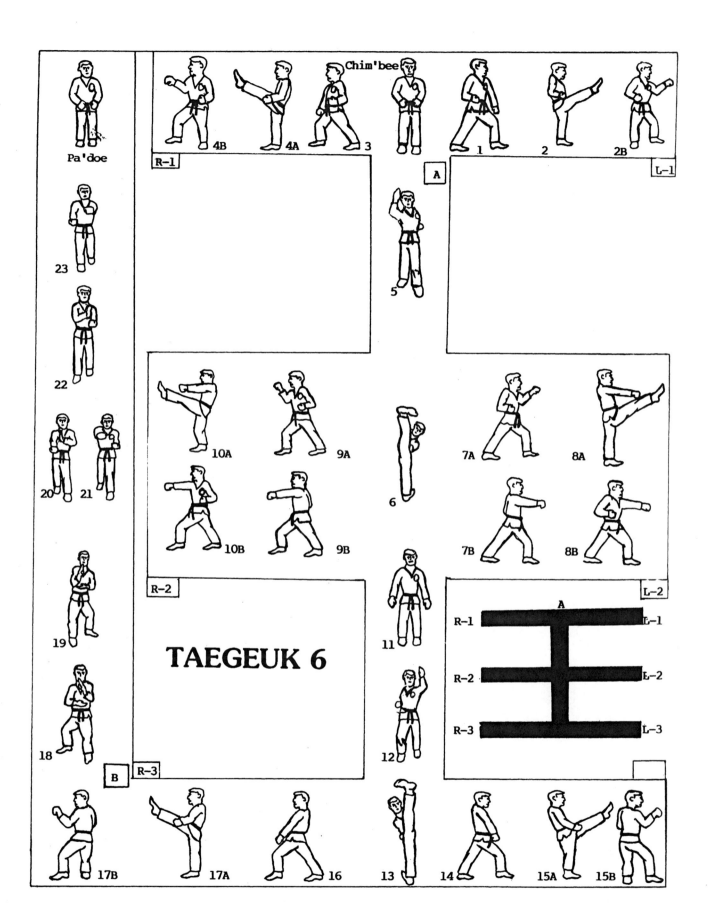

TAEGEUK CHIL CHONG
(7)

Taegeuk Seven, symbolizing ancient philosophy of the Mountain. This form introduces the cat stance and a variety of two-handed techniques. The knee strike and the crescent kick are found in this form. The walking stance is seen once again in movements 20 and 22.

1. REVERSE PALM BLOCK (L) CAT STANCE
2.   A) FRONT KICK (R)
   B) Replace kicking foot-INSIDE BLOCK (L) CAT STANCE
3. REVERSE PALM BLOCK (R) CAT STANCE
4.   A) FRONT KICK (L)
   B) Replace kicking foot - INSIDE BLOCK (R) CAT STANCE
5. LOW SUTO FIGHTING STANCE (L)
6. LOW SUTO FIGHTING STANCE (R)
   Step left foot into CAT STANCE
7. REVERSE PALM BLOCK with guide arm (L) TIGER STANCE
8. (Twisting) REVERSE BACKFIST (L) TIGER STANCE
9. REVERSE PALM BLOCK with guide arm (R) TIGER STANCE
10. (Twisting) REVERSE BACKFIST (R) TIGER STANCE
11. Slide left foot into right foot -
    Circular motion with right fist-
    Coming into left palm then up.
12.   A) REVERSE LOW BLOCK/MIDSECTION BLOCK COMBINATION (L)
    B) LOW BLOCK/REVERSE MIDSECTION BLOCK COMBINATION (L)
13.   A) REVERSE LOW BLOCK/MIDSECTION BLOCK COMBINATION (R)
    B) LOW BLOCK/REVERSE MIDSECTION BLOCK COMBINATION (R)
14. DOUBLE HAMMER BLOCK (L)
15.   A) KNEE STRIKE (R)
    B) DOUBLE UPPERCUT (R) Cross-legged Stance
16. Step back with left foot into LOW CROSS BLOCK
17. DOUBLE HAMMER BLOCK (R)
18.   A) KNEE STRIKE (L)
    B) DOUBLE UPPERCUT (L) Cross-legged Stance
19. Step back with right foot into LOW CROSS BLOCK (L)
20. OUTSIDE BACKFIST (L)
21.   A) INSIDE CRESCENT KICK into palm (R) Fall into straddle Stance
    B) ELBOW STRIKE into palm (R)
22. Slide back foot up - BACKFIST (R)
23.   A) INSIDE CRESCENT KICK into palm (R) Fall into Keimo Stance
    B) ELBOW STRIKE INTO PALM (L)
    C) OUTSIDE SUTO BLOCK (L) KEIMO STANCE
24.   EXTENDED PUNCH (R) GIYUP KEIMO STANCE

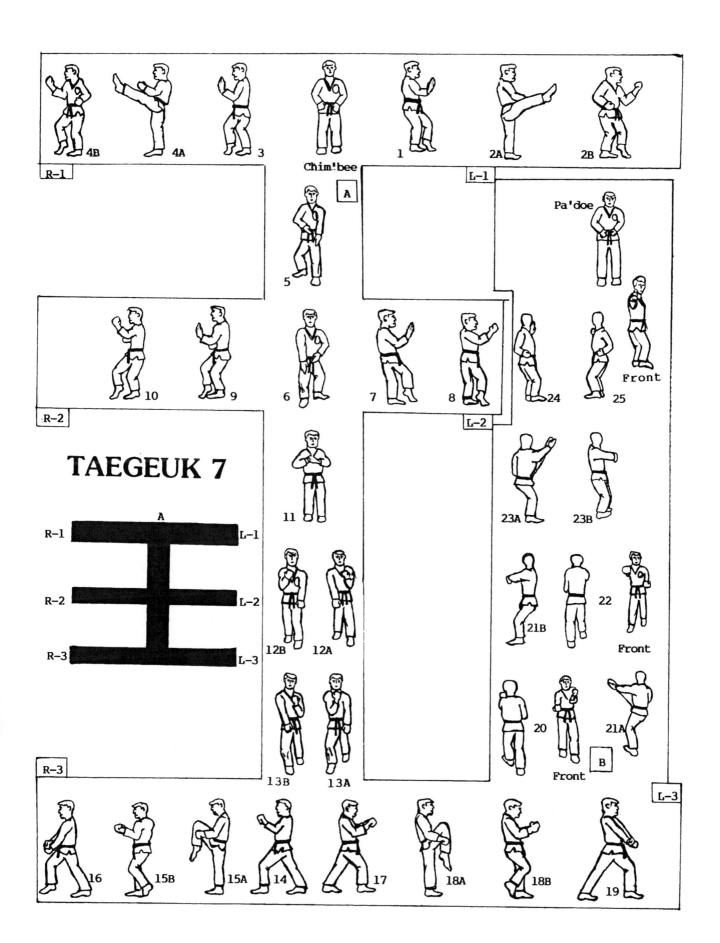

TAEGEUK PIL CHONG
(8)

Taegeuk Eight follows the ancient principle of Earth. This is the last of the Taegeuk forms and should be performed with the precision and total concentration of mind and body learned in the previous forms. It is the culmination of all prior techniques combined with variations of these movements including the reverse square stance and jump front kicks. Dynamic tension is also to be found in this form.

1. A) FIGHTING STANCE (L) (Forward palm out)

    B) Slide forward foot over into forward stance REVERSE PUNCH (L)

2. A) Front foot-JUMP FRONT KICK (L) GIYUP!
    B) INSIDE BLOCK
    C) REVERSE PUNCH (L) foot ,Rt. hand
    D) PUNCH (L)

3. PUNCH (R)

4. LOW BLOCK/REVERSE OUTSIDE BLOCK COMBINATION

    REVERSE SQUARE STANCE (L)

5. Shift into L-STANCE

    REVERSE UPPERCUT/Dynamic tension (L)

6. A) Step left foot over right foot

    B) LOW BLOCK/REVERSE OUTSIDE BLOCK COMBINATION

    REVERSE SQUARE STANCE (R)

7. Shift into L-STANCE

    REVERSE UPPERCUT/dynamic tension (R)

8. Step right foot back down middle-FACE CHOP (L)

    Shift forward foot over

9. REVERSE PUNCH (L)

10. A) FRONT KICK (R) Replace right foot then step back with left foot.

    B) PALM BLOCK (R) Step left foot up to CAT STANCE

11. FACE CHOP (L)

12. A) FRONT KICK (L)

    B) REVERSE PUNCH (L)

13. PALM BLOCK (L) CAT STANCE

14. FACE CHOP (R) CAT STANCE

15. A) FRONT KICK (R)

    B) REVERSE PUNCH (R)

16. PALM BLOCK (R) CAT STANCE

17. LOW SUTO FIGHTING STANCE (R)

18. A) FRONT KICK (L)

    B) JUMP FRONT KICK (R)

    C) INSIDE BLOCK (R)

    D) REVERSE PUNCH (R) GIYUP

19. OUTSIDE SUTO BLOCK (L)

20. A) REVERSE ELBOW (L)

    B) REVERSE BACKFIST (L)

21. PUNCH (L)

22. OUTSIDE SUTO BLOCK (R)

23. A) REVERSE ELBOW (RO

    B) REVERSE BACKFIST (R)

24. PUNCH (R)

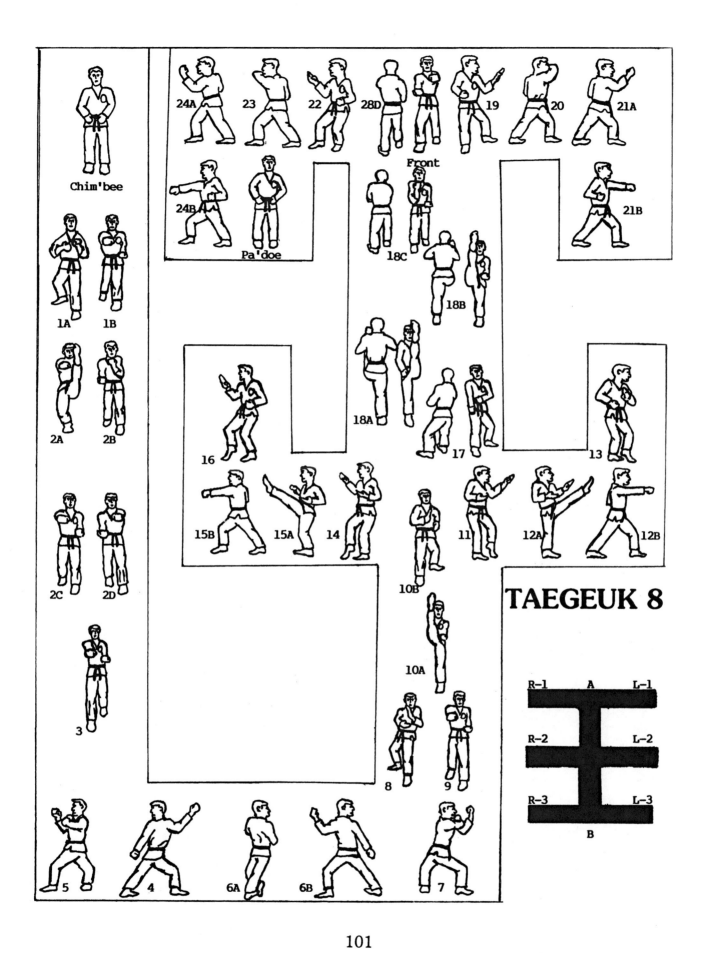

Become an Expert in Poomse and you will become a champion over all your physical weaknesses.

The following are rules to remember before one can perform the formal exercises properly, in order to receive the maximum benefit from the execution of the many techniques within the structure of each form:

Rule No. 1   Execute each position cleanly and completely, before going on to the next movement.
Rule No. 2   Be satisfied with your performance. If necessary, repeat it several times until it feels good and until you feel confident while applying the technique.
Rule No. 3   Breathe regularly throughout the Form, using the diaphram rather than the chest, and exhale simultaneously with the last action in each movement.
Rule No. 4   Keep your fists tight and your body relaxed. Throughout the Forms, your body should be relaxed, except at the instant you complete each block, punch, strike, and kick. Your whole body should then be locked into tense focus on that action.
Rule No. 5   While standing at attention before beginning the Form, take a deep breath and exhale slowly while you think only of what you are about to do. Create a strong sense of concentration, rid your mind of all distractions and place all outside problems deep in the back of your mind.

Forms should be practiced diligently before the student attempts serious free sparring, so that his techniques are as perfect and accurate in actual fighting as they are in solo training. The Forms are designed purposely so that the student should develop patience through repetition.

Student: Why learn Forms?
Soldier: Why learn to march?
Instructor: Through learning you will come to know.

PART FOUR
ONE-STEP SPAR

The principle of One-Step Spar, also known as Semi-Spar, is to come as close as possible and even touch an opponent without inflicting the slightest pain. The one advantage of this method is that the attack is always a high punch unless designated by the instructor in charge. Therefore, the defending student can concentrate more on the counter-attack. This method also simulates a combative situation without the risk of serious injury. Chung Do Kwan is known to have the most power and precise one-step sparring techniques of any other form of Karate. Practice devotedly with pride.

ONE-STEP SPARRING SETS

This unique training method was created by the U.S. Chung Do Kwan Association primarily for the beginning students.

Prior to the introduction of the One-Step Sparring Set System, it was very difficult for the beginning student to memorize one of TKD/Karate's most important part of training that emphasized "controlling the blow." Also referred to as "semi-spar" by some schools, One-Step Spar has many other objectives that are extremely important while training in karate.

Set Nos. 1 through 10 introduce the most common hand technique used throughout the world in karate. Set Nos. 11 through 20 introduce the most common foot techniques used in combination with Set Nos. 1 through 10. Set Nos. 21 through 40 are identical as Set Nos. 1 through 20 except that the opposite hand or foot is used when applying them. EXAMPLE: If you applied Set Nos. 1 through 20 while standing in front of a mirror, you image in the mirror will have executed Set Nos. 21 through 40.

As a beginning student, you will be expected to practice Advanced One-Step Spar only after you have perfected your One-Step Sparring Sets required for your next rank.

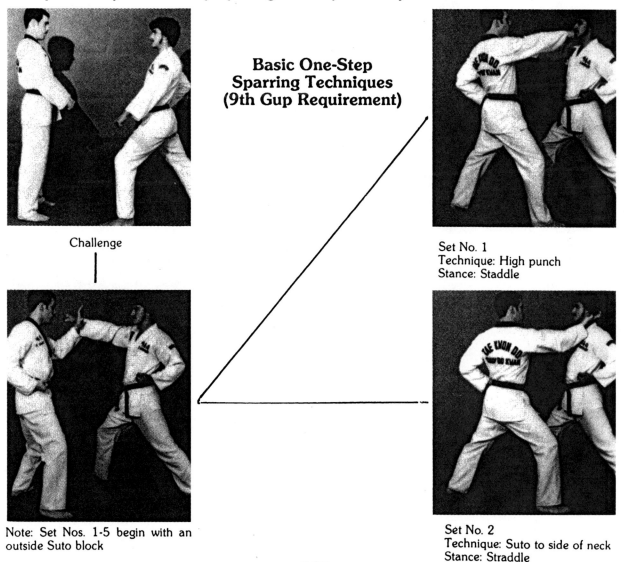

Basic One-Step Sparring Techniques (9th Gup Requirement)

Challenge

Note: Set Nos. 1-5 begin with an outside Suto block

Set No. 1
Technique: High punch
Stance: Staddle

Set No. 2
Technique: Suto to side of neck
Stance: Straddle

Block

Set No. 3
Technique: Palm strike to chin
Stance: Straddle

Set No. 4
Technique: Horizontal elbow strike
Stance: Straddle

Set No. 5
Technique: Spear hand
Stance: Straddle

Set Nos. 6-10 begin with an inside forearm block.
Stance: Straddle

Set No. 6
Technique: Vertical back-fist
Stance: "T"

Set No. 7
Technique: Side chop to side of neck
Stance: "T"

Note: Step to left side in straddle stance, block with left arm

Set No. 8
Technique: Combination of two punches to flank, one punch to head
Stance: Straddle

Set No. 9
Technique: Foreward elbow thrust
Stance: "T"

Block

Set No. 10
Technique: Foreward elbow thrust
Stance: "T"

Followed by: Pivot elbow strike to rear

Combination One-Step Sparring Techniques
(8th & 7th Gup Requirements)

Block

Front-snap kick

Set No. 11: High Punch

Set No. 12: Chop to side of neck

Set No. 13: Palm-strike to chin

Block

Front-snap kick

Set No. 14: Vertical elbow strike

Set No. 15: Spear-hand to the throat

Side-kick

Inside forearm block followed by:

Set No. 16
Technique: Back-fist
Stance: "T"

Set No. 18
Left side-kick

Set No. 17
Technique: Side-chop
Stance: "T"

Technique: Step to left block with left forearm   Combination two punches to flank, one punch to head

111

Set No. 19   Side-kick   Inside forearm block   Foreward elbow thrust
                                                                   Stance: "T"

Set No. 20   Round-kick to sternum   Side-chop to cerebellum
Step to left with left forearm block
Stance: Straddle

CREATIVE ONE-STEP SPAR
(GREEN AND BLUE BELT REQUIREMENT)

Creative one step spar consists of creating ones own sparring techniques with the fundamentals equivalent to his/her rank. The one step sparring should be precise, concentrating on combinations and focus.

 —  —

FRONT KICK BLOCK

 —  —

OUTSIDE CRESCENT KICK BLOCK

Advanced One Step Spar

Advanced one step spar consists of developing sparring techniques incorporating combinations of advanced kicking techniques, take downs, jumping kicks, as well as striking from various angles.

INSIDE CRESCENT KICK BLOCK

ADVANCED ONE STEP SPAR

Combinations

Hook Kick

Pass-by

Slap-Round Kick

 —  —

 —  —

 —  —

116

PART FIVE
FREE STYLE SPARRING

Free Style Sparring or Free Sparring is the ultimate in advanced TaeKwonDo training. The Japanese word often used in tournaments is "Kumite". The Korean word is "Da'lyum". Sparring begins when two students show respect by bowing to each other, falling back into a fighting stance, and then at the command of the instructor, beginning to spar. They are free to execute any TaeKwonDo technique provided they refrain from hard body and face contact. Emphasis is placed strictly on "controlling" the blow in order to prevent injury or pain. Two good Tae Kwon Do students should be able to free spar for an extended period of time, unleasing many flurries of kicks, punches and chops to all vulnerable areas. After the match is completed, neither should have the slightest bruise or have suffered the slightest pain. Such practice sessions reflect the true "skill" and "art" of a well trained Chung Do Kwan student.

Unlike other forms, styles or schools of TaeKwonDo/Karate which teach their students to "pull punches", Chung Do Kwan teaches the student to control the punch, kick or chop. Perhaps body contact is made, but with the proper control applied there is no pain or injury.

We believe that the practice of continued pulling of the punch can easily become a force of habit. If the time should ever arise that a student has no alternative left but to defend himself, it is very possible that he will "pull his punches" which could result in his defeat or perhaps even his death. The TaeKwonDo student must quickly realize that this control would only apply during training sessions and not in self-defense on the street. Within a Tae Kwon Do class the student is surrounded with an atmosphere of *friendship, brotherhood and learning.* There is no intent to do bodily harm and therefore, under the watchful eye of the instructor, the student is quite conscious that he must control his attacks and counter-attacks against his fellow student.

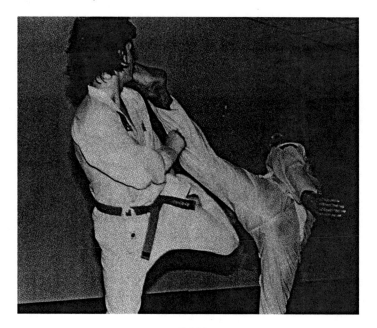

You will also be instructed by your ranking superiors in TaeKwonDo/Karate to react to an aggressor most *effectively* by reading his inadvertent signals which "telegraph" his attacks. This will be taught to you during your special classes concerning street defense.

Place a TaeKwonDo student in a street fighting situation and his habit of controlling force in practice sessions will allow him to adjust instantly to hostile reality with however much force may be necessary. In defending himself, he will subconsciously switch to an uninhibited mode of fighting, relying on the reflexes developed during his TaeKwonDo training. The result will be his VICTORY. (NOTE: the defensive techniques of TaeKwonDo will only work properly when the student has complete control over his faculties.)

Free sparring can also be explained as, "a simulated combative situation with only the empty hands and bare feet for weapons in the attacks and counter-attacks."

When first introducd to free sparring (fourth to sixth week of training) the student is taught that there are two tools. Both are very important. Tool #1 is the "fake". Tool #2 is the technique (an intended strike with the hand or foot).

He is also told that there are: "Three Categories of Weapons" used while free sparring. Weapon #1 is your brain, for you must try to out think and out maneuver your opponent. (Remembering past experiences can be of great help towards the improvement of your free sparring ability). Weapon #2 is your feet. Since it is a fact that the legs are 10-20 times stronger than the arms, your legs are your second most important weapon. Weapon #3 is your hands, used in faking, blocking, and when at close range with your opponent, striking with various punches and chops. (NOTE: There are seventeen weapons on one hand of a skilled TaeKwonDo student.)

By combining the knowledge obtained in TaeKwonDo training with the proper use of the tools and weapons used in free sparring, the TaeKwonDo student becomes one of the world's most knowledgeable beings in the 'ART" of self-defense.

NOTE: Free Style Sparring is explained in more detail in Chapter 4.

CATEGORIZING FREE STYLE SPARRING

For the first time, the author attempts to separate the many different training methods of free style sparring. It is believed that no one has documented the varieties of sparring within the martial art of karate and TaeKwonDo.

#1. No-Contact Sparring: This simply means that both opponents refrain from any contact except that created by blocking techniques. A practice used primarily during the beginning stages of training.

#2. Controlled Contact: This is the first step into advanced sparring. Both opponents take great care when delivering the blows and concentration is on "controlling" each delivery.

#3. Light/Medium Contact: More speed and power is used during this training method as the student becomes more confident with the basic punching and kicking techniques. At this point the instructor must be present to closely supervise each match and offer his constructive criticism when needed in order to aid in the prevention of injuries. The extent of body contact must be a mutual understanding between the two students. It is normally a custom to allow the lower ranked student to choose and/or gage the degree of contact to be made.

#4. Full-Contact: This method is not used during any training session and is discouraged by most instructors unless proper protective gear is worn. Body armor, such as chest protectors, groin protectors, shin and fore-arm guards and hand and foot protectors, are required and, if heavy contact to the head is allowed, proper head-gear is a must. Many weeks and months of special body conditioning is necessary, in addition to road-work to increase one's stamina. To become an "artist," a Black Belt or just a good student in TaeKwonDo/Karate, this type of free style sparring is absolutely unnecessary and should be left to those who wish to become professional combatants.

#5. Multiple: Two or more against one spar using controlled sparring rules. This method indeed sharpens all areas of defensive reflex training and can prepare a student for a "real-life" situation. This method is usually used when a student is being examined for a higher rank.

#6. Weapons: Simulating a "street fighting situation," a fake knife, club or chain is used by someone who also is wearing protective gear. Medium-contact normally is the rule. Also used for examination purposes.

#7. Technical: A method used by "highly skilled" students who may execute many jump/flying kicks, which are very difficult to control, also using combinations of foot-sweeps and take-downs. Using medium to heavy contact, but based on skill level, very few if any techniques actually make contact on target. Used only within the Black Belt ranks and/or during Black Belt examinations.

#8. Tournament/Competition: This is done when a student must combine all that his instructor has taught him and his own common sense and experience.

How are injuries prevented? This is a very common question asked by laymen. The author believes that there are two basic reasons why two students can punch and kick at each other with speed and power, and yet not inflict any serious injury on one another. First, we must remember that there is no intent to inflict injury. Second, all contact sparring is supervised by a qualified instructor who, by closely observing the actions of the students, can take corrective steps when the amount of contact or force appears inappropriate to the skill level of the students. This careful supervision eliminates injuries before they occur. In addition, the student is trained to "roll with the punch or kick" and learns to expand his peripheral vision which aids him in blocking an attack that would otherwise be outside his line of vision. By combining these elements, you now have a unique explanation and answer to the question that is on the minds of most potential students and/or parents. "Isn't karate dangerous? Can someone get seriously injured practicing karate?" There must be proper training and supervision. Yes, as in all body contact sports there is always risk of injury, but in the field of martial arts, it is the knowledge, credentials and reputation of the instructor that limits the potential of accidental injury.

PART SIX
THREE IMPORTANT EXERCISES

What is the need for calisthenic exercise? There are several reasons for the many calisthenics of Tae Kwon Do training.

#1. In order to properly execute the hundreds of defensive techniques, the student must condition his/her body or suffer painful injury by pulling or straining a muscle if the body is not in good physical condition.

#2. By strengthening the muscles throughout the body especially in the chest, back, and abdomen areas, a student can absorb a much harder blow to that area, such as in free sparring. A Tae Kwon Do student can absorb a blow to the solar plexus that would normally send a non-student crumbling to the ground.

#3. The strict discipline experienced by the Tae Kwon Do student during a class session strengthens the mind. Therefore, the various exercises tone the body muscles thereby strengthening and conditioning the total physical structure.

#4. The strengthening of muscles throughout the body will allow the student to deliver a kick, punch, or chop eight to ten times as forceful as the average non-student. These are only four reasons for the "finishing exercises". There are many more.

RUNNING IN PLACE

SIT UPS

PUSH UPS

SPARRING AND SELF DEFENSE

4

"WHAT IS A FAKE?"

The word fake is defined in the dictionary as "an intimidation or false pretense." These explanations are as close as one can come to simplifying the description of a fake in free style sparring. The fake is the most important part of free sparring; without it you have nothing. You might as well kick a brick wall, and that is almost how it feels when a kick is solidly blocked because there was no fake executed prior to the delivery of the technique. "A fake is 50-80% extension of a technique just prior to executing the actual strike or kick." If a fake looks like a fake, nothing has been accomplished, since the opponent will not attempt to block a kick or strike if he thinks the offensive motion will not touch him. Therefore, there will be no opening in his defense. (NOTE: Your opponent's defense is his ability to block your techniques.) A student of Chung Do Kwan must realize that if he plans to strike or kick high, he must first fake low; if he plans to strike or kick low, he must first fake high. It is also very important that a fake be made to the farthest corner from the area which he actually intends to strike. A good Chung Do Kwan student can have complete control over his opponent simply by executing the proper fakes. Since the legs are the most powerful weapons in self-defense, the student would be wise to fake with the hands in order to make an opening for his feet. This can work out in the opposite order but only after much experience in the art of free style sparring. When a student's fakes begin to look like actual techniques in the eyes of his opponent, the student's ability in free sparring will begin to accelerate upward.

In this Volume, I will only illustrate one of many basic fakes. Photos A and B demonstrate the simple application of the side-chop (suto) to the back of my opponent's neck while free sparring. It is very important that you notice two things: #1. My left hand has been positioned to check and block any attack to the kidney or rib cage. #2. I have placed my right leg knee-to-knee to my opponent's right leg (photos B & C), therefore I can check or block a side-kick or round-kick simply by lifting my knee. An experienced Chung Do Kwan student can detect that specific point at which he can instantly change the fake into an actual technique. For example, if the opponent does not block a continued fake, the student can reverse his strategy by actually carrying through with the fake, which will then become a technique. One this has been done and contact has been made with the opponent, the opponent will immediately attempt to block any attack to the area most recently struck. He will do this on impulse when he thinks the same technique will be repeated. When the opponent raises his arm(s) to block the attack, (which is actually a fake), an opening is made in his defense allowing the side-kick to be applied which scores the point and/or defeats the adversary. (NOTE: Photos C & D.)

A

B

C

D

THE THREE MOST IMPORTANT WEAPONS OF THE HUMAN BODY

If you were asked, "What is the first weapon of the human body when it comes to self defense?" you would probably answer, "The hand or foot." This is incorrect! It is the human mind or the "controller" of all technical human body movement. The leg and foot are second because the leg is ten to twenty times more powerful than the arm. And, believe it or not, the hands are number three. Still, the arms are very important, not only because the hands depend on them to function properly, but because the arms are considered the "defense" of the human body. Using circular movements, the arms can block any attack to the upper and lower parts of the body with very little effort. The simple low, mid-section, high and outside blocks taught to the TaeKwonDo beginner are all that he needs to be able to intercept an attack to his body from any angle. Assuming a "T stance" and using these basic blocks, the student is able to block any attack high or low to any part of his body with very little effort.

BASIC BLOCKING TECHNIQUES

Low Block [Square Stance]   **Low Block [T-Stance]**

Mid-section Block (square stance)

Mid-Section Block (T-stance)

High Block (square stance)

High Block (T-stance)

Outside Block

Outside Block

OTHER BLOCKING TECHNIQUES

Inside Block

Palm Block also called check block

Crossed Wrist Block
This technique can also be used for blocking a higher attack.

Knee/Leg Block
Used for blocking kicks below the belt. Senior ranked students must not use this technique while sparring a lower ranked opponent since it can cause painful leg bruises to the attacker.

TAEKWONDO AS A FORM OF SELF DEFENSE

The law states that persons have the right to defend themselves and their property by whatever means necessary to ward off an assailant. Therefore, the knowledge of TaeKwonDo/Karate can be used, but only to the extent necessary to prevent or stop a physical assault or damage to personal property. At that point, one's actions must stop, for the law also states that one has no right to punish another person. Once the assault has been thwarted, the defender would become the assailant if he were to continue to kick and punch.

In the many years of training and research, the author has classified the four ways in which anyone can defend himself:

#1. By using a weapon of some kind, such as a firearm, knife or club.

#2. Striking with the empty hand or kicking with shoes on or off. This could actually be called TaeKwonDo or Karate regardless of the proficiency with which the technique was delivered.

#3. Throwing or tripping. The Japanese call such a means of self defense Judo which means gentle way. That is hard to believe, since it is a long, hard drop over a person's hip or shoulder, especially when the objective is to have the opponent land on his back or head.

#4. Twisting limbs and joints, causing tremendous pain which forces the assailant to surrender. Even though Judo has arm bars and various take downs while twisting limbs, it is Akido and Hapkido that throws an assailant across a room with a simple twisting of joints and pressure applied to vital areas of the body, rendering the opponent helpless.

Right from the beginning of his interest and training in the Oriental Martial Arts, the author discovered that the Korean form or style of Karate (TaeKwonDo) was by far the easiest to learn and the most effective, as well as practical. For this reason he geared all his efforts to one particular school (or training system) called TaeKwonDo Chung Do Kwan, also referred to as one of the original forms of modern day Karate.

Let us analyze all four of these methods of self-defense:

A. Naturally using method #1 seems to be the simplest, but you risk the chance of breaking the law by concealing a weapon. You also risk the chance of killing someone unnecessarily or getting yourself killed with the "show of too much force".

B. Even though Judo is considered only a sport throughout much of the world, today it is also looked upon as a very effective means of self defense. By simply "grabbing ahold" of your enemy, you are able to throw him to the ground. However these apparently simple techniques take many months and years of training to execute with confidence in an actual combat situation.

C. As in Judo, one must be very close to the enemy to effectively execute the techniques of Akido (Japanese), and Hapkido (Korean). Much patience and a long period of training are required to perfect these twisting and throwing techniques. Both also demand accurate knowledge of the body's pressure points.

D. It does not take much common sense to realize that the secret of defending yourself is to keep your assailant away from you. This can be done most effectively by kicking, giving you a distance equal to the length of your leg between you and your enemy. It is a fact that with only a few lessons from a reputable school of TaeKwonDo, a man or woman of any age or size can learn to strike out with his/her hands and feet into designated vulnerable areas of the body, making it the simplest Oriental Martial Art that anyone can be taught.

"CHANNELS OF DEFENSE WITHIN THE SUBCONSCIOUS"

A well-trained martial artist soon discovers that he has three states of mind which function automatically. Here we will call them "channels."

The first channel, the green channel, is the state of mind that one experiences when in a friendly, warm atmosphere among family or friends. There is no fear of any harm being done to anyone in these surroundings; no anger or harsh feelings exist among anyone present.

The second channel is instantly turned on when one finds himself in a strange and uneasy atmosphere, perhaps a dark alley where an emergency may arise. This may be called the "yellow" or "alert" state of mind, when one immediately prepares to take whatever action is necessary to ward off an attack or prevent any harm from coming to him. He walks very cautiously straining to focus on any unusual movement.

Channel three, "red" or "danger," instantly turns on when an immediate threat is directed at him. It is at this time that adrenalin flashes through the body, and he knows that he must not allow it to block his judgment of the situation. Whatever amount of training in self-defense and self-control he has had from the day of his birth to the moment of crisis will determine the outcome of this emergency situation. Good judgment and common sense are the two main factors that will assist him in resolving this situation with the least amount of injury to both parties. According to the law, "Every man has the right to defend himself, his property, or his loved ones by any means that would aid in warding off an assailant." One must learn how to defend himself and loved ones. However, once the assailant has stopped his attack, the defender has no right to "punish" him further, and if he does so, the defender then becomes the "assailant."

"THREE WORLDS OF FIGHTING"

The three "channels of the subconscious" is a term I use to explain the three different types or "worlds of fighting," using the word "world" to mean: "A state of mind that a person puts himself in when in combat with another."

In formal TaeKwonDo class sessions, a good Instructor never uses the words "fight, hurt, kill, break, crush, gouge, tear or rip" when referring to the result of a strike or blow delivered during sparring. All blows must be properly controlled, so that absolutely no injury occurs. Thus, we have the first world of fighting, in which there is neither fear, anger or intent to do bodily harm. Fear and anger do not exist in this world. Formally, this is not fighting at all. As you read further, notice the explanation of fighting compared to sparring.

The second world of fighting is "Tournament, Free-Style Sparring." Here one attempts to out-maneuver, out-think and ultimately, out-score his opponent. As in sparring at the toe'chang (school), there is no fear or anger and no intent to do bodily harm. However, it is also much different from the learning relationship of sparring one's teacher or a fellow student. In competition, one has challenged himself to measure his technical knowledge of TaeKwonDo sparring against another student approximately equal in skill and who may be someone from a different school that he has never seen before. He feels that the whole world is looking at him, even though there may be only a handful of fellow students present. Here, the fear is not of being injured or hurting the opponent, but it is the fear of losing and not living up to his Instructor's expectations. Eighty percent of winning at competitive TaeKwonDo/Karate events is "experience" and a thorough knowledge of the rules and the system of scoring points. One cannot evaluate his performance as a student or his skill in self-defense by how well he competes in tournaments. Such an evaluation would not be fair to him or his Instructor.

World three of fighting is the ultimate challenge, a confrontation in the street or in a place that you have a right to be, but someone has violated your rights. At this point, a strong sense of discipline could easily solve this problem and prevent any harm from coming to either person. A true martial artist would use all other means before resorting to the use of his hands and feet in self-defense. He would try to act as calmly as possible, placing a barrier between himself and the words that were intended to insult him and to stir his adrenaline to such a high pitch that he would react in panic and begin punching without thinking, which is exactly what his opponent would want to happen. By hiding his fear and reflecting his calmness, he very slowly begins to weaken his opponent with each word, telling him that all this nonsense could be settled in a more amicable way, without resorting to a street confrontation. Naturally, if words are not effective, one applies only the amount of force needed to stop any further unnecessary bumps, bruises, and blood shed. A good rule to follow that would prevent anyone from finding himself in this type of situation is: "Avoid people, places, and things that cultivate such senseless activities."

Now let us try to imagine that you failed to follow the above rule and you are faced with a situation in which a stranger is now standing in front of you, insulting you, etc. "What in the world am I going to do?" should be your first question as your mind races 1,000 miles an hour to try to find an answer. There is a unique system that I have taught my student to use when faced with this situation. The system is actually a series of questions that one must ask himself, provided that he has the time, naturally. These same questions can be asked whether there is a weapon involved or not. If there is a weapon, it would be very wise to think out each question more thoroughly. The questions are a follows:

1. What am I doing here?
Meaning: What is the reason for this?
2. Is he for real?
Meaning: Does he really intend to do harm to me if I don't do what he asks? Is he serious?
3. Can I walk/run away from this?
Meaning: Is there a route of escape?
4. Is what he is asking worth the possibility of blood shed if I don't give him what he wants:
Meaning: Should I call his bluff?
5. Am I prepared psychologically and physically to fight him?
Meaning: Am I willing to risk injury and do I have confidence in striking or kicking back at him?

Let us now create some logical answers and analyze each question:

Question 1. If you have an answer to "What caused this situation", you may have a good opportunity to "talk" your way out of the situation entirely. You must, first of all, be as calm as possible and don't show alarm, since that may be exactly what he wants, only to scare you. When he realizes that he has not accomplished scaring you, he may have second thoughts and become uncertain or unsure of himself, giving you an opportunity to take charge of the discussion or make a powerful and accurate move to gain escape. Facial expressions sometimes tell the whole story of one's feelings. Be careful of yours and study his.

Question 2. If your answer is "Yes", and he has no weapon, and you are skilled in a form of martial arts, I personally feel that you have wasted too much time at this point and should be on "Channel Three" "(Red-Danger"), prepared to strike. If he has a weapon, give some serious thought and wait for your most perfect opportunity. "I suggest that you move only if your life is at stake. To shed your blood for money or other material goods is, I feel, to have used poor judgement."

Question 3. You would be plain foolish to stand there and let someone threaten you and continue to insult you if you have many avenues of escape available. If it is in the public view of bypassers, attempt to join them or call out to someone using a fictitious name; even go so far as to try to ignore your assailant as you walk away. Once you have broken away, run directly to the nearest sign of life, such as a store or house with lights on. At that point, make your report to the police.

If your back is to the wall and your assailant blocks the only route of escape, your problem becomes more serious, especially if no one else is around. In the case of a "women's self-defense situation", a chapter in this book encourages the lady to yell her head off in an attempt to get the attention of anyone within hearing distance. At this point, I suggest that serious consideration be given to the next question.

Question 4. This question cannot be properly answered unless you know exactly what it is that your assailant wants. For the ladies reading this book, I suggest that you turn to the chapter on "Women's Self-defense", immediately, before you actually find yourself in a real situation like this one. For the men, it would depend on (1) whether he had a weapon and (2) the nature of the assailants demand. It becomes a very personal decision between you and the man that has threatened you. If you have no intentions of giving him what he wants, we then come to the final question.

Question 5. Do you realize that only about two percent of the male population of the world knows how to make a fist properly, not counting those well trained in a martial art? For women it is approximately one-half percent. The very first principle taught to anyone learning how to defend himself is how to make a fist properly. Therefore, since only that small percentage of people may be naturally talented enough to defend themselves, without training it could be very disastrous for someone to give a "false inpression" and ultimately make awkward and ineffective movements that would only make him more vulnerable to his assailant. That is where the old saying "He knows enough karate to get himself killed" comes from. If you are not prepared to fight because you simply have no knowledge of self-defense or no confidence in the use of it, it is time to use your knowledge of "human nature" and to try your best to communicate with your assailant. Be sincere and act as though you understand him and try to bring the traumatic situation down to a low pitched discussion. Once you have done that, explain the serious consequences that he will face if he does not start using his own common sense. Once the talking begins, don't stop.

If your answer to this question is "yes" and you have the confidence to strike back at your assailant , it is suggested that you stall a while until the assailant places himself in a position were you can strike with your hardest and most powerful blow. All forms of martial arts teach their students self-defense and attempt to simulate street confrontations, but remember, these are nothing compared to the "real thing". Other than your hands and feet, the best weapon you will have is your self-control and self-discipline, which will allow you the good judgement you need so as not to make the situation any worse than it really is.

Here is what the ancient Masters of the Oriental Martail Arts felt about fighting and self-defense:

They placed peace and quiet over victory. They would avoid violence and force. They would not stop force, but re-direct it. They believed it was more important to find ways to preserve rather than destroy.

They lived by the following code:
1. Avoid rather then check
2. Check (block) rather then hurt
3. Hurt rather then maim
4. Maim rather then kill

"For all forms of life are precious, nor can any be replaced." Thus the philosophy of ancient Masters stresses respect for life.

Korean "Subak", a very old name for Tae Kwon Do Chung Do Kwan, was renowned the deadliest form of fighting known to man. The followers of Subak avoided violence, but also took an oath upon their own life, stating, "If one must resort to his knowledge of Subak in self-defense, he must kill his enemy without inflicting pain, or he will suffer a painful, lingering death himself."

Today, when the true Black Belt straps that piece of black material around his waist prior to instructing his students, he feels a deep, sincere feeling within his soul that he has truly earned the respect and title of a "Black belt".

Regardless of the style of karate that he may belong to, the true Black Belt does not place himself in situations that could possibly call for him to resort to his knowledge in self-defense.

In the military, the officers are commissioned as "Gentlemen" by the act of Congress. So, too must, the Chung Do Kwan Black Belts take an oath of allegiance to recieve his commission as a "gentlemen" in the Martial Art of Tae Kwon Do from the U. S. Chung Do Association.

VULNERABLE AREAS

The human body has a great many vulnerable areas, or so-called "chinks in the armor." Blows, kicks, or pressure directed at or applied to these areas may cause pain, disablement, unconsciousness, and even death. As depicted in Chart 2, the most vulnerable areas of the body are located on or near the "midline," the imaginary line that bisects the body. Blows delivered to this "midline" area, either front or back, generally have a much greater effect than blows which are delivered elsewhere.

Knowing where to strike blows and where to apply pressure is just as important as knowing how to strike the blows and how to apply the pressure. As a rule, the untrained person will direct his blows to his opponent's head or face. This is the exact place most people expect to get hit and, as a result, this is the area they intend to protect. In protecting the head and face, most individuals forget about protecting the large areas of the trunk. The trunk contains a great many vulnerable areas and it is much more difficult to protect than the head and face. This is due largely to the fact that it is a much bigger area and hence easier to hit, and also because it is very difficult to avoid blows aimed at the trunk without moving the feet. Blows aimed at the head and/or face can be avoided rather easily by ducking or slipping the head, and this action does not require moving the feet.

As a general rule, a counterattack should not be directed to the opponent's head and face, but to the "midline" area of the trunk, such as the liver, solar plexis, pit of stomach, floating ribs, the soft tissue area of the abdomen, or the groin.

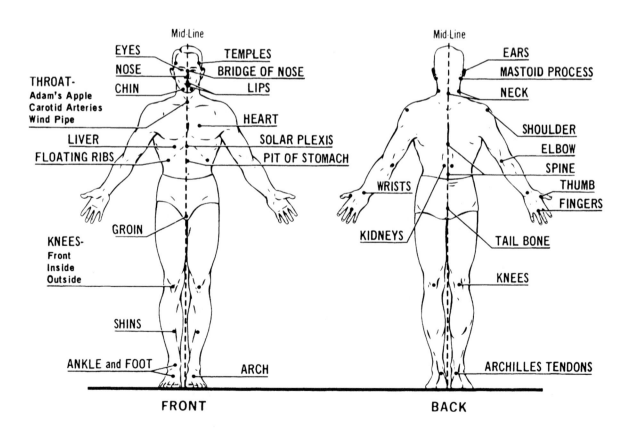

U.S. CHUNG DO KWAN ASSOCIATION

Patches, Emblems & Logos used by this Association

UNITED STATES CHUNG DO KWAN ASSOCIATION EMBLEM

Designed in 1967 by Grandmaster Edward B. Sell, this emblem very closely resembles the world's first Taekwondo association, the Korea Taekwondo Association in Seoul, Korea.

Significance of each color:

- **White** — Purity of mind, heart, body, and spirit.
- **Gold** — Represents the Master. The U.S. Chung Do Kwan Association was founded by an American Master. Also a tribute to our U.S. Chung Do Kwan Masters.
- **Blue** — Represents freedom.
- **Red** — Represents the blood that was shed to obtain our freedom.
- **Black** — Death. A tribute to those who have given their lives for our freedom.

Significance of design:

- **Fist** — Universal emblem of Taekwondo and Karate.
- **Shield** — Self-protection.
- **Two circles** — Universe and the circle of life.
- **Two stars** — Life now and life after death.
- **Korean writing** — Chung Do Kwan.
- **Stripe behind fist** — Represents a Black Belt.
- **Four flower petals** — Grandmaster Sell was only a 4th degree Black Belt when he organized the U.S. Chung Do Kwan Association. The petals are from the national flower of South Korea.

ORIGINAL CHUNG DO KWAN EMBLEM

WHAT IS CHUNG DO KWAN?

Let's begin by looking at the history of modern day Taekwondo. Taekwondo was not taught in Korea for many years because it was under a dictator rule of government. The only people who practiced Taekwondo were those who were taught by their father, one on one. In 1941, a gentleman by the name of Won Kuk Yi (Lee) founded a unique method of teaching Taekwondo to a group of students rather than "one on one." He was a Professor at one of the colleges in Korea and received permission from the government to teach to selected men.

He called his method of teaching "Chung Do Kwan" which can be translated several ways, such as "The Great Blue Wave" and many other translations relating to man's first source of power "the force of water." Have you ever stood by the ocean and watched the waves come in? If you have, I'm sure you'll agree that it is a spectacular display of power. The waves can get very violent and even tear down buildings, land, trees, whatever may get into their paths. Grandmaster Sell prefers to use the translation "a mighty wave smashing against a rocky shore," because the power of water striking against any living or lifeless form on earth will win. Today, Chung Do Kwan is one of Taekwondo's strongest Taekwondo training systems. Mr. Won Kuk Yi has been titled as a Great Great Grandmaster and Founder, and is presently retired in the U.S. acting only as an advisor in the world movement of Taekwondo.

In 1967, Grandmaster Sell founded the American branch of the Taekwondo Chung Do Kwan Association, with the emphasis on strict discipline, shifting of body weight at the point of impact, and many other teaching techniques that would inspire the American student. Today, Grandmaster Sell is known as a pioneer of American martial arts. Being one of the first successful American organizations, he created the "scale model" for Taekwondo organizations that is responsible for setting high standards and developing not only black belts, but also leaders throughout the United States.

HISTORY OF U.S. CHUNG DO KWAN ASSOCIATION

On March 25, 1967 Air Force Staff Sergeant Edward B. Sell received an Honorable Discharge from the U.S. Air Force after serving eight years on active duty. His one hope and dream was to some day open his own Korean Karate (TaeKwonDo) Studio and build it into a national organization, so that others may benefit from his newly found "Way of Life".

In the summer of 1967, it was decided that Trenton, Michigan would be the site of his first studio. Many repairs and much remodeling were needed. With the help of his three brothers Tom, Ray, and Ron, the studio was opened in a very short time with the very limited funds that were available.

August 18, 1967 the Trenton Karate Studio held its first class session with twenty-five enthusiastic beginners under the command of Master Instructor Edward B. Sell.

The strict discipline and "hard core" training molded these white belts into hard fighters whose reputation began to spread throughout the East Coast shortly after entering their first tournament in June 1968, when eight students brought home twelve 1st and 2nd place trophies and the Overall Club Championship Trophy. The impressive association patch worn on all the students' uniforms began to be feared by many competitors of other Karate Schools.

Today, Grandmaster Sell's dream has been fulfilled, as the U.S. Chung Do Kwan Association is indeed a National Organization and is growing even beyond Grandmaster Sell's expectations. Grandmaster Sell is reaching out and helping Taekwondo Instructors who have been abused or misused by offering them a "home." Each Instructor becomes a part of the team as we work together to expand Taekwondo and it's growth throughout the world.

It is felt by Grandmaster Sell that the Martial Arts is still in its infancy in the United States. Teaching, Demonstration, Conducting Seminars, and Tournaments are ways in which Master Sell and the U.S. Chung Do Kwan Association are promoting the arts. The future of the martial arts remains with all Black Belts who dedicate themselves to the principles and teachings of TaeKwonDo and Karate.

Taekwondo Seminars and Conferences

Since 1967, Grandmaster Sell has given at least two large seminars each year. In the early stages of organizing these events, each student brought their own tent, cooking utensils and all other materials needed to survive in the wilderness for a whole weekend.

The goal of the U.S. Chung Do Kwan Association is to train leaders for the future. In order to do that, we must share our knowledge with others and live up to their expectations as teachers, mentors and role models.

The U.S. Chung Do Kwan Association has schools in most states throughout America. The Sell Team, (Grandmaster Sell, Grandmaster Brenda, and their son Robby) travel nearly six months each year visiting their chartered schools, teaching Taekwondo, Leadership principles and performing Taekwondo demonstrations in churches, military bases, prisons and schools.

In 1994 The Sell Team began their **Soaring Eagle Tours**. These tours take them crisscrossing America in their motor home called Eagle 1. Prior to this time, the students came to geographically selected locations to receive this specialized training. Today, the annual Soaring Eagle Tour travels to key locations throughout the country for one day seminars making it more convenient for students, black belts, and instructors to attend. Each seminar is filled with fun, excitement, and motivation. The impact of these seminars is so dynamic that students of all ages and ranks look forward to attending year after year.

In 1999 while driving down the highway in Eagle 1, Grandmaster Sell felt challenged by God to train the U.S. Chung Do Kwan members who want to make a difference in this world by developing a plan to help stop the decay of our society through a program entitled the "Morality Revolution." (You can read more about this at the end of Chapter 10). Leaders who want to make a difference can now be trained and mentored by The Sell Team through the teaching principles of the U.S. Chung Do Kwan Association and powerful biblical leadership principles.

U.S. Chung Do Kwan Training Conferences

Each year, the U.S. Chung Do Kwan Association also hosts a three-day training conference for students and black belts of all ranks. Instructors and Masters come from all over the country to share their knowledge and experience. Each conference has from 20-60 workshops. The student is given a list of the workshops and chooses their own itinerary based on the topics offered. Each year the conferences continue to grow as people leave challenged, inspired, and motivated.

U.S. Chung Do Kwan Association
30th Anniversary Celebration
1967-1997

Looking back through the years, it is evident that we were created to touch the lives of others in a positive way. The year 1997 was filled with celebration. In the next few pages we would like to share some of the highlights that led up to and were included in this historical celebration. Thank you to all the students, Black Belts, and Masters who have stood by our side and supported our vision with your dedication and commitment to Grandmaster Sell and the U.S. Chung Do Kwan Association.

1960-1969
History of Edward B. Sell & Formation of an American Taekwondo Association

1961-1967 — TaeSooDo Chung Do Kwan student at Osan Air Force Base, Korea

1963 — First American to compete in the Korean National Championship.

1966 — First American to receive Taekwondo Certificate of Merit from Korea Taekwondo Association

1967 — First American to receive 4th Degree Black Belt. First American to receive the Master Instructor Degree. Formation of Korea Taekwondo Association of America. Trenton, Michigan

1969 — Developed the Instructors Degree certification system. Authored America's first Taekwondo training manual.

(Above) Edward B. Sell in training at Osan AFB, Korea
(Below) E.B. Sell makes history as the only foreigner to compete in the 1st Korean National Championship.

The birthing of a dream to teach Americans this unique form of self defense starts at the opening of Master Sell's first school, August 17, 1967

1970-1979
Building the Foundation of the U.S. Chung Do Kwan Association

1970 — Professor Brenda begins training.

1972 — EBS - First American to be awarded the International Master by the WTF. BJS – Awarded Black Belt.

1973 — EBS – U.S.A. Team Coach for the 1st World Taekwondo Championships. World Bronze medal winner, Ray Sell, brother of EBS. Authored one of America's best selling textbooks, *Forces of Taekwondo*.

1974 — EBS - First American to be awarded International Referee Certification. Committee member for formation of WTF. Headquarters moved to Ann Arbor, MI.

1975 — Association name changed to United States Chung Do Kwan Association. EBS appointed member of WTF Technical Committee.

1976 — EBS - International Referee, 1st World Games Seoul, Korea.

1977 — BJS - First female to be awarded WTF International Referee Certification.

1978 — Brenda J. Sell is awarded the 4th Degree and Master rank.

1979 — USCDKA Headquarters moved to Lakeland, Florida.

(Above) Master Sell is certified as America's first International Referee. (Below) Brenda J. Sell being examined as the first female International Referee.

International Referee Master Sell referees at the 1st World Games.

1980-1989
Major Expansion Programs Begin

1981 — The Sell Team, an International Christian Taekwondo Demonstration Team was formed. (This is a separate, non profit organization)

1983 — Brenda Sell is invited to Korea by the WTF officials to give advice concerning the debut of International female competition at the 1st Pre World Games Seoul, Korea.

1985 — Edward B. Sell is ordained as a Christian minister at Cypress Cathedral, Winter Haven, FL by Full Gospel Fellowship in Dallas, Texas.

1987 — EBS receives 8th Dan by WCDK. Grandmaster Hae Man Park appoints Master Edward B. Sell to Grandmaster.

Brenda J. Sell is appointed as International Referee for the 1st Women's World and 8th World Taekwondo Championships in Barcelona, Spain. This was the first time females were allowed to referee on an International basis.

1988 — Grandmaster Sell is appointed to the Public Relations Committee for the Olympic Games – Seoul, Korea.

1989 — The Sell Team is invited by the U.S. Army Chaplains to minister and perform Taekwondo Demonstrations in Germany and Czechoslovakia.

1989 — World Taekwondo Federation awards Letters of Citation to outstanding USCDKA Instructors recommended by Grandmaster Sell.

The Sell Team, Christian Ministry had its debut on International Television on the famous 700 Club.

Below:
Grandmaster Sell, Great Grandmaster Uhm, Uoon Kyu, and Grandmaster Hae Man Park at the 1988 Olympics.

International Referee Brenda J. Sell in Barcelona, Spain for the 1st Women's Championships.

1990-1999
The Decade of Growth

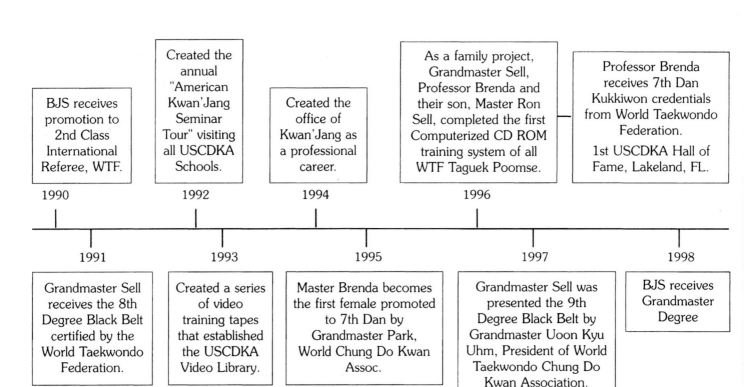

- **1990** — BJS receives promotion to 2nd Class International Referee, WTF.
- **1991** — Grandmaster Sell receives the 8th Degree Black Belt certified by the World Taekwondo Federation.
- **1992** — Created the annual "American Kwan'Jang Seminar Tour" visiting all USCDKA Schools.
- **1993** — Created a series of video training tapes that established the USCDKA Video Library.
- **1994** — Created the office of Kwan'Jang as a professional career.
- **1995** — Master Brenda becomes the first female promoted to 7th Dan by Grandmaster Park, World Chung Do Kwan Assoc.
- **1996** — As a family project, Grandmaster Sell, Professor Brenda and their son, Master Ron Sell, completed the first Computerized CD ROM training system of all WTF Taguek Poomse.
- **1997** — Grandmaster Sell was presented the 9th Degree Black Belt by Grandmaster Uoon Kyu Uhm, President of World Taekwondo Chung Do Kwan Association. USCDKA 30th Anniversary Celebration
- **1998** — BJS receives Grandmaster Degree
- Professor Brenda receives 7th Dan Kukkiwon credentials from World Taekwondo Federation. 1st USCDKA Hall of Fame, Lakeland, FL.

Below: Grandmaster Hae Man Park Awards Brenda J. Sell her 7th Dan.

Students are highly involved in the excitement of Grandmaster Sell's lectures. Below: The debut of the World's 1st Taekwondo CD ROM written by Master Ron Sell, performed by Prof. Brenda and directed by Grandmaster Sell.

U.S. Chung Do Kwan Association Hall of Fame

Below is the original text of the 1996 Hall of Fame Program written by Grandmaster Sell.

BLACK BELT HALL OF FAME

For nearly twenty years, I have dreamed of having an awards banquet where my lovely wife, Professor Brenda and I could salute our most faithful members, associates, students, Masters, Instructors and friends. The time has come. We are blessed to have so many faithful students who share our vision. With this event, there will be plenty of excitement as the names of each inductee is announced and the category that he or she will be placed in history as their names are recorded in the 1996 USCDK Black Belt Hall of Fame.

A few speeches and special words will be said, the special awards will be presented as symbols of the many years of hard work, sacrifice and dedication of each inductee. The event will soon turn into a memory. As each honored member takes their award and places it on display, my wife and I simply ask that each time you look at it, you remember that you are appreciated and loved in a very special way. Also, never forget that as a member in good standing, we as leaders of this unique association will be there if you need us. You are very special to us and we would like to see our relationship with you flourish and last a long time.

God's blessings have been overwhelming to us. Every prayer, hope, and dream has come true in our lives. God has a purpose and a plan for each of us. Our ultimate goal is to find and live that purpose and plan to the fullest. The greatest promotion anyone can receive is our entrance into the Kingdom of God. This promotion is not based on talents or abilities, but rather a commitment to our Lord and Savior. What greater gift could anyone give than their life? That's what Jesus did for us! His life was a life of giving, the same principle we as Instructor's live by. It is so easy for a good martial artist to become a Christian because the discipline, respect, and commitment factors are already developed. It is my heart desire that each of you experience the same peace, success, and acceptance that I have found in Jesus Christ.

You have been an intricate part of the success and growth of this association. Your support of the Kwan'Jang and his office, helps us stay on track with the visions, goals and values of this American owned and operated martial arts institution. Lives are being touched, character traits are being strengthened, and thousands of young people have mentors to look to. These mentors are the leaders of this association, the Black Belt Instructors and Masters who care about them. You, the USCDK Black Belt are making a difference in this world. The many family and friends that support our Black Belts can also make a difference in this world by locking onto the USCDK Association purpose and motto, "To Give Strength to the Weak, Confidence to the Timid and Spiritual guidance to those who seek after God!"

U.S. Chung Do Kwan Association Hall of Fame

1996 HALL OF FAME INDUCTEES

Master Mark Begley, Ernest & Wilma Begley, Mr. John Burt, Mr. Andrew Chaney, Master Carol Covensky, Mater James Covensky, Ms. Judy Haase, Mrs. Keva Harris, Master Ricky Harris, Mr. Richard Hernandez, Miss Julie Howell, Mr. Charles Knight, Master Frank Loureda, Master Richard McDowell, Mr. Adriano Mendoza, Mr. Lazaro Moreno, Mr. Alex Packard, Mr. Van Palmer, Grandmaster Hae Man Park, Mr. Kenny Pompliano, Master Michael Reidhammer, Mr. Mike Sabo, James & Cheryl Sexton, Professor Brenda J. Sell, Raymond C. Sell, Mr. Robert E. Sell, Master Ronald E. Sell, Master Robert Smith, Master Edward Ashley Stell, Mr. Michael Thompson, Miss Stephanie Thompson, Master Melanie Wyatt, Master Chet West, Mr. Scott Wisneski, Master Peter Yelorda, Mrs. Margaret Young, Mr. Paul Zucnick

1997 HALL OF FAME INDUCTEES

Master Mark Begley, Mr. Drew Chaney, Master Daniel Coblentz, Master James Copeland, Mr. Keith Coker, Mr. Richard Craven, Mr. Clinton J. Dees, Mr. Danny Dorton, Ms. Susan Edwards, Master Bill Evans, Mrs. Susan Fisher, Mr. Dustin Graham, Mrs. Margaret Glessner, Master Judy A. Haase, Master Keith Hafner, Mr. Theron Higgins, Miss Melissa A. Hillyard, Mr. Jason Landaas, Mr. Texas Phillips, Master Ron Sell, Mr. Jason Smith, Mr. Jerry Stanback, Mr. Buddy & Ty Thomas, Mr. Michael Thompson, Mr. Randolph E. Thompson, Mr. Jeremy W. Waibel, Master Melanie Wyatt, Mrs. Shanda J. Woolman

THE IMPORTANCE OF PRACTICING AT HOME

There is an old saying, "Practice Makes Perfect." The problem with this statement is that practice only makes perfect if you practice right. If you practice mistakes repeatedly you simply embed the mistakes into your muscle memory and motor encoding. However, practicing correctly really does lead to perfection. The USCDKA has many training aides including DVD's that will help you on your pathway of personal excellence. Check the website regularly for updates.

As a student, your enthusiasm can be expressed by the amount of time you practice on your own at home. The student must realize that the purpose of a formal class session is to give the Instructor and opportunity to review what you have practiced and to make corrections in all areas. Therefore, a student who attend class comes to learn, not necessarily to practice.

A living room, bedroom, basement, hallway ore backyard can become a temporary toe'chong (training area). Be creative and have fun! I can clearly remember practicing my forms hundreds of time while working a late night shift guarding aircraft on an isolated runway in Korea. Any size that works for you is good (just be sure that all breakable objects are moved).

Without a good self-training program you may become discouraged with yourself. Constant repetition is the pathway to perfection and you are only as good as the efforts of your practice.

Grandmaster Mark Begley demonstrated the results of continuous practice as he breaks two stacks of concrete simultaneously. However, breaking boards, concrete, or bricks should only be attempted with the supervision of a certified instructor. Photo: March 1995

U.S. Chung Do Kwan Association Uniform Code

During the organizations stages of the United States Chung Do Kwan Association (formerly known as the Korea Taekwondo Association of America, 1967-77), the founder, Grandmaster Edward B. Sell, spent much time in designing the necessary patches, emblems and logos that would identify this American association from all others. He also had to determine the placement of these patches on the original uniform. The appearance of the United States Chung Do Kwan Association toe'balk (uniform) was designed to create incentive and enthusiasm, plus a slight air of competition and envy among lower belts and members of rival organizations. He also designed the distinction between each Gup (student) rank and inspired many other Instructors throughout the country to do the same.

Please Note: *Before reading much farther into the uniformity code of United States Chung Do Kwan Assoc. I wish to explain an important break-through in my career. In 1991, I opened our membership to other schools and organizations and gave more freedom to school owners. This freedom allows others to express teaching methods and uniform codes of their own. Today, in order to become a "Blue Book School", no less than 80% of the uniform code and operational structure must be in accordance with this textbook. It pleases me to say, that most of our schools are Blue Book classified.*

THE TOE'BALK

FOR THE STUDENT

Training Uniform consists of three parts:

A. White Jacket, "V" neck

B. 1-1/2" belt

C. White loose pants

NOTE: The new jacket and belt design was introduced by the World TaeKwonDo Federation, Seoul, Korea, in 1978. This new martial arts uniform was designed to be worn only by TaeKwonDo practitioners.

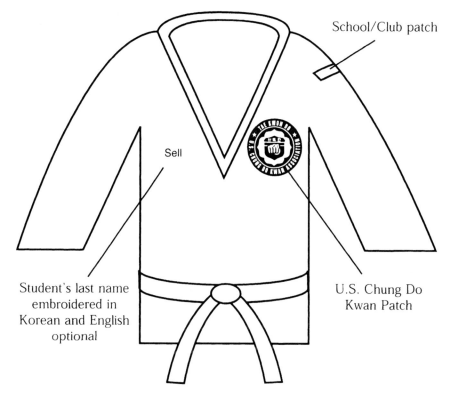

Sell

Student's last name embroidered in Korean and English optional

School/Club patch

U.S. Chung Do Kwan Patch

FOR THE BLACK BELT

Sr. Instructors and Masters wear a gold trim sewn on the black v-neck.

Grandmaster E. Sell

The rank of a black belt is signified by the number of gold stripes at the end of the belt. Master belt: A black belt with 3" broken gold stripes the length of the belt. Grandmaster belt: A black belt with a gold stripe the length of the belt.

Instructors' patch signifying the degree earned.

U.S. Chung Do Kwan Patch

Each stripe represents four years continuous training. A double stripe at the end of the sleeve represents a certified Master. Black Belt stripes are black, Master stripes are black and gold.

A full color U.S. Chung Do Kwan Logo is worn on the back of the uniform with the school name on the outside of the lower portion of the logo.

PANTS:
USCDKA certified Instructors may wear black pants.

USCDKA Sr. Instructors may wear black pants with a white stripe trimmed with gold on the pant legs.

USCDKA Masters may wear black pants with a gold stripe trimmed with white on the pant legs.

SPECIAL NOTE: The lapel of a Junior or Teen black belt 15 years old and under, is red and black following the rules of the World Taekwondo Federation, Seoul, Korea.

U. S. CHUNG DO KWAN ASSOCIATION RANK SYSTEM

DESCRIPTION OF BELTS

10th Gup..White Belt
9th Gup...Yellow Belt
8th Gup...Gold Belt
7th Gup..Orange Belt
6th Gup...Green Belt
5th Gup..Purple Belt
4th Gup..Blue Belt
3rd Gup...Red Belt
2nd Gup...Brown Belt
1st Gup...Brown Belt with Black Stripe through the Center
1st Degree...Black Belt
*1st Poom...Red/Black
1st Degree (Dan) Confirmed/Certified...Black Belt with Name and Korean Writing in Gold Letters
2nd Degree...Black Belt with Two Gold Bars

Note: Some schools may vary in belt colors, however the gup system should be the same skill level.
*Poom is a Taekwondo do term for a black belt student under 15 years old.

THE BELT AND RANK EXPLANATIONS

The belt or "dee" worn by the student off Taekwondo not only holds the toe'balk (uniform) tightly around the waist for greater freedom of movement, but it is a symbol of accomplishment. It is indeed an achievement to be qualified to wear any color of belt.

Although the Western culture has been accused of making Martial Arts belt an egotistic symbol, the original objective of the colored belt system was to identify each student's skill level which is a training aid for the instructor.

Let us compare the various ranks in the U.S. Chung Do Kwan Association with the grading system in our public schools. The beginner ranks (10th-7th Gup) are the elementary school level. The intermediate ranks (6th – 4th Gup) are the junior or middle school level. The advanced ranks (3rd – 1st Gup) are the high school level. The Black Belt ranks (1st – 3rd Dan) are the college level. The 4th Dan Black Belt begins the Masters Degree.

It should be the goal of every student to someday be a black belt.

"A Black Belt is a White Belt that never Quit!" Edward B. Sell

U.S. CHUNG DO KWAN ASSOCIATION TESTING REQUIREMENTS

9th Gup through 1st Dan

The gup students are students below the rank of black belts.

There are many different belt colors and some schools and organizations place the order of belt promotions differently, so it is important to know both your belt color and gup rank.

There are three groups of students in the gup ranks:

Beginner	10th gup, White Belt
	9th gup, Yellow Belt
	8th gup, Gold Belt
	7th gup, Orange Belt
Intermediate	6th gup, Green Belt
	5th gup, Purple Belt
	4th gup, Blue Belt
Advanced	3rd gup, Red Belt
	2nd gup, Brown Belt
	1st gup, Brown Belt with a black stripe.

The two biggest enemies are "lack of self confidence and discouragement".

Do not allow either of these obstacles to overcome you.

NOTE: The various colors of belts, requirements and curriculum that follow are only suggested. Our "Blue Book Schools" are the traditional schools that adhere to at least 80% of the curriculum. Blue Book schools and Christian Taekwondo University (CTU) schools may add to, but not take away from the requirements.

REQUIREMENTS NEEDED TO GRADUATE THROUGH THE BEGINNER STAGES:

9TH GUP YELLOW BELT
Belt of Encouragement

NINTH (9TH) GUP- Yellow Belt:

1. Customs and courtesies of Taekwondo plus school rules.
2. Six Basic Stances plus the Walking Stance and fighting stances
3. 1 – 7 of Basic Fundamentals, focus on square stances (pg 63-66)
4. One Step Spar: One step sparring sets #1-5 (pg 104-106)
5. Oral Quiz- Subject: Class rules; TKD rank; USCDKA patch. (pg 21-26, 138, 151)
6. Portfolio check

Alternative Children's Curriculum

1. Customs and courtesies of Taekwondo plus school rules.
2. Stances: Attention, Bow, Chimbee, Square Stance, Straddle Stance
3. 1 – 7 of Basic Fundamentals, focus on square stances (pg 63-66)
4. One Step Spar: One step sparring sets #1-5 without a partner (pg 104-106)
5. Oral Quiz- Subject: Class rules; TKD rank; USCDKA patch. (pg 21-26, 138, 151)
6. Short Essay: How Taekwondo Helped Me So Far
7. Portfolio check

BEGINNER STAGE

CONGRATULATIONS!!! You have now started on a wonderful journey in Taekwondo. Many people only dream of learning this exciting martial art, but YOU are doing it.

The two enemies of a beginner are: (1) discouragement and (2) lack of confidence. Don't let either of these enemies stop you from achieving your goals.

ORAL QUIZ FOR 9TH GUP CANDIDATES

1. There are four sitting positions for students while in uniform — True False
2. Gym shoes are allowed on the training area — True False
3. The Taekwondo uniform is called a Toe'Chong — True False
4. You may address you Instructor by his/her first name if you are related — True False
5. You may chew gum while practicing Taekwondo — True False
6. A tardy student must wait to be recognized by the Instructor before asking permission to join class — True False
7. According to our Textbook there are four rules why we do not wear shoes while training in a formal class session — True False
8. You do not have to come to the position of attention each time you are approached by your Instructor — True False
9. You may carry your uniform draped over your shoulder when entering the training area — True False
10. You may wash your belt each time that you wash your uniform — True False
11. A student may wear black pants when he becomes a brown belt — True False
12. The Taekwondo training system that you are being taught is called Chung Do Kwan — True False
13. Pa-doe in Taekwondo terms means "Ready position" — True False
14. There are five colors in the U.S. Chung Do Kwan Association emblem — True False
15. The fist in the center of our emblem is from the left hand — True False

Answers: 1. False, 2. False, 4. False, 5. False, 6. True, 7. True, 8. False, 9. False, 10. False, 11. False, 12. True, 13. False, 14. True, 15. False

8TH GUP GOLD
Belt of Excitement

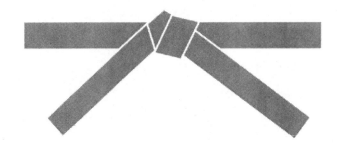

EIGHTH (8TH) GUP- Gold Belt

1. Basic fundamentals #1 – 11, *new 8 – 11 (pg 63 – 68)
2. Basic Fundamentals not illustrated in this text book:
    a. Inside Block- Walking Stance and "T" Stance
    b. Hammer Block- Walking Stance, Square and "T" Stance
3. Poom'se/Form: Taeguek Il Chong (pg 84-87)
4. One Step Spar: One step sparring sets #1 – 10, *new 5 – 10 (pg 104 – 108)
5. Oral Quiz- Subject: same as 9th gup plus Taekwondo weapons (pg 5-15, 21-26)
6. Portfolio Check

Alternative Children's Curriculum

1. Stance: t-stance (both 50/50 and 80/20)
2. Basic Fundamentals #1-11, plus hammer block
3. Kei-bon #1
4. One Step Spar: sets 1 10, *new 5-10 with a partner
5. Oral Quiz
6. Portfolio Check
7. Short Essay – My Goals in Taekwondo

ORAL QUIZ FOR 8TH GUP CANDIDATES:

1. The walking stance is actually a short forward square stance. True False

2. According to our newest textbook there are seven basic stances. True False

3. Yuk'Jin is a TaeKwonDo term meaning "shout". True False

4. There are only four basic weapons on one hand. True False

5. The elbow is the only weapon that can be used against an assailant at close quarters. True False

6. Karate is a Korean word meaning TaeKwonDo. True False

7. A square stance is two shoulders long in length, but a walking stance is about one shoulder length. True False

8. According to our new textbook there are 26 "personal" striking weapons on the human body. True False

9. The shoulder can be used as a blocking weapon. True False

10. The United States Chung Do Kwan Association (USCDKA) was founded by an American. True False

11. Rule #2 of "true cleanliness" is "Clean Body " - Practice good personal hygiene True False

12. There are 7 belt levels in the U.S. Chung Do Kwan student ranks. True False

13. The TaeKwonDo term Gup (also spelled Geup) means "a skill level within the student ranks". True False

14. The World TaeKwonDo Federation headquarters is located in Seoul, Korea. True False

15. A defensive reflex is the ability to block an attack without having to think about it. True False

Answers:
1. True, 2. False, 3. False, 4. False, 5. False, 6. False, 7. True, 8. True, 9. True, 10. True, 11. False, 12. False, 13. True, 14. True, 15. True.

7TH GUP ORANGE
Belt of Inspiration

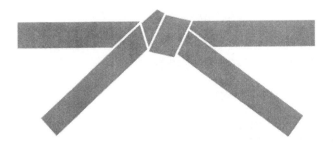

SEVENTH (7TH) GUP- Orange Belt

1. Basic Fundamentals, #1 – 15, *new 12 – 15 (pg 63 – 71)
2. Poom'se/Form: Taeguek Ee Chong (pg 84-85, 88-89)
3. One Step Spar: One step sparring sets #1-15, *new 11 – 15 (pg 104 – 110)
4. Oral Quiz- Subject: Taekwondo history; USCDKA founder; TKD customs and courtesies (pg 6 – 10, 23- 26, 31 – 38, 152 – 153)
5. Portfolio Check

Alternative Children's Curriculum

1. Basic Fundamentals, #1 – 15, *new 12 – 15 (pg 63 – 71)
2. Kei-bon 2, Kei-bon 3, Kei-bon 4
3. One Step Spar: One step sparring sets #1-15, *new 11 – 15 (pg 104 – 110)
4. Oral Quiz- Subject: Taekwondo history; USCDKA founder; TKD customs and courtesies (pg 6 – 10, 23- 26, 31 – 38, 152 – 153)
5. Portfolio Check

ORAL QUIZ FOR 7TH GUP CANDIDATES

1. There are traces of Taekwondo as far back as 37 B.C. in the form of murals and giant carvings. True False

2. Taekwondo became the most poplar during the Silla Dynasty. True False

3. A Kwan is actually a school that teaches the art and science of Taekwondo. True False

4. By 1980 there were 27 different styles of Korean martial arts. True False

5. The first Taekwondo organization to have world-wide recognition was called the "Korea Taekwondo Association". True False

6. In 1975 the President of Korea declared Taekwondo a "national sport". True False

7. Grand Master Edward B. Sell formed the U.S. Chung Do Kwan Association in 1967. True False

8. Grand Master E. B. Sell was the first person outside of the Korean Nationality that was ever awarded 4th, 5th, 6th, 7th Degrees of Black Belt. True False

9. The first and only foreigner to compete in a Korean National tournament, called the Presidential Championship was 3rd Degree Black Belt, Edward B. Sell in 1963. True False

10. It is tradition to never let your belt touch the floor. True False

11. If you are tired and dressed in a Toe'Balk, it is permissible to stretch out and take a short nap while waiting to be tested or at a large tournament. True False

12. When in doubt about a rule or traditional custom, it is wise to ask a senior student before approaching your Instructor. True False

13. A Grand Master is the teacher of Masters. True False

14. The Black Belt is a symbol of being a Champion over all your weaknesses. True False

15. When awarded the 6th Gup Green Belt, a person is no longer called a "beginner". True False

Answers: 1. True, 2. True, 3. True, 4. False, 5. True, 6. False, 7. True, 8. True, 9. True, 10. True, 11. False, 12. True, 13. True, 14. True, 15. True

REQUIREMENTS NEEDED TO GRADUATE THROUGH THE INTERMEDIATE STAGES

SIXTH (6TH)GUP- Green Belt, Belt of Talent
1. All Basic Fundamentals, including #16 thru #28 (pg 63 – 75)
2. Poom'se/Forms (pg 84 – 85, 88 – 91): Taegeuk Som Chong
3. One-Step Spar: # 1 – 20, *new 16 – 20, (pg 104 – 112)
4. Free Style Sparring, (pg 117 – 121)
5. Written/Oral Quiz:- Subject; Basic Taekwondo (Korean) terminology; USCDKA history; what is a Master? (pg 21- 26, 31- 55)
6. Essay: 150 words "Why are you taking Taekwondo and how has it helped you thus far?
7. Portfolio Check

Alternative Children's Curriculum
1. All Basic Fundamentals, thru #17 (pg 63 – 72)
2. Poom'se/Forms (pg 84 – 85, 86-87): Taegeuk Il Chong
3. One-Step Spar: # 1 – 20, *new 16 – 20, (pg 104 – 112)
4. Free Style Sparring, (pg 117 – 121)
5. Written/Oral Quiz:- Subject; Basic Taekwondo (Korean) terminology; USCDKA history; what is a Master? (pg 21- 26, 31- 55)
6. Essay: 150 words "Why are you taking Taekwondo and how has it helped you thus far?
7. Portfolio Check

INTERMEDIATE STAGE

CONGRATULATIONS!!! Upon being awarded a Green belt (6th gup), you have now graduated to the Intermediate Stage of training. During this stage you will polish the basic concepts and begin to build on them. A wide range of training aides are available through your Instructor and online www.uscdka.com to help you in your quest for excellence. If you haven't already begun to enter tournament competition and participate in demonstrations and seminars, you will need to now. These out of class opportunities will be very instrumental in giving you the tools to become a "well-rounded" student. Keeping your portfolio up to date will be very helpful as you continue your journey to Black Belt.

ORAL QUIZ FOR 6TH GUP CANDIDATES

1. A Master is a teacher of Black Belts. True False

2. A Master must be at least a 4th Degree Black Belt and must meet other specific requirements according to the USCDK rules. True False

3. One of the qualifications to be a Kwang Jang is that the person dedicated most of his adult life to the art of teaching Taekwondo as a career. True False

4. A Kwan'Jang is the highest position anyone can receive in the art and science of TaeKwonDo. True False

5. The U.S. Chung Do Kwan Association was founded in 1967. True False

6. The TaeKwonDo term Pa'doe means "sit down". True False

7. Yuk'jin shult means "Parade Rest" True False

8. Poomse simply means "forms" True False

9. Grandmaster Sell started the U.S. Chung Do Kwan Association by opening his first school in a small town outside of Detroit, Michigan. True False

10. A simple English translation of a Kwan'Jang is Grand Master. True False

11. A Master is a teacher of Black Belts. True False

12. The U.S. Chung Do Kwan President moved the Headquarters Office to Lakeland, Florida in 1969. True False

13. A Dee is a term used for uniform. True False

14. Com'mult means to "line up and adjust your uniform". True False

15. The Grandmaster and Kwan Jang' of the World Chung Do Kwan Association is the Honorable Un Kyu Uhm, who resides in Seoul, Korea. True False

Answers: 1. True, 2. True, 3. True, 4. True, 5. True, 6. False, 7. True, 8. True, 9. True, 10. True, 11. True, 12. False, 13. False, 14. True, 15. True.

5TH GUP PURPLE
Belt of Motivation

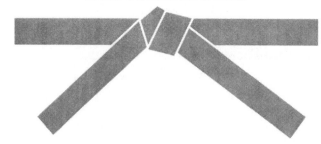

FIFTH (5TH)GUP- Purple Belt

1. Basic Fundamentals #1 – 26, *new 21 – 26 (pg 63 – 80)
2. Poom'se/Forms (pg 84 – 85, 90 - 93): Taegeuk Sa Chong
3. One-Step Spar: #1-40, *new 21 – 40, *new 10 advanced, , (pg 104 – 116)
4. Free Style Sparring: Controlled contact, (pg 117 – 121)
5. Written/Oral Quiz- Subject: Six parts of a Taekwondo Class, (pg 58 – 122)
6. Portfolio check

Alternative Children's Curriculum

1. Basic Fundamentals #1 – 20, *new 18-20 (pg 63 – 75)
2. Poom'se/Forms (pg 84 – 85, 88-91): Taegeuk Ee Chong, Taegeuk Som Chong
3. One-Step Spar: #1-40, *new 21 – 40, *new 5 Creative One Steps, , (pg 104 – 113)
4. Free Style Sparring: Controlled contact, (pg 117 – 121)
5. Written/Oral Quiz- Subject: Six parts of a Taekwondo Class, (pg 58 – 122)
6. Portfolio check

ORAL QUIZ FOR 5TH GUP CANDIDATES

1. According to our textbook there are five parts of a formal "TaeKwonDo class. True False

2. If you are late it is not necessary to stretch out if class has already begun. True False

3. The term "Dul" means "#9 count". True False

4. It is not necessary to count in Korean in order to conduct a formal class. True False

5. The word "Dan" is pronounced as "Don". True False

6. Eel-bon-da-dee-un means to "free spar". True False

7. **Poomse training helps a student develop precision, control, and self-discipline.** True False

8. It is the responsibility of the senior student to conduct an inspection. True False

9. Japanese word for Poomse is Kata. True False.

10. When coaching a beginner you must be forceful and very critical of all errors. True False

11. If a beginner is extra sharp, you should teach him poomse his first day. True False

12. **It is very important to stretch prior to a class or strenuous workout.** True False

13. As a coach it is important that you become good friends with the beginner that you have been assigned to. True False

14. As a coach you have the authority to discipline the beginners. True False

15. **According to our textbook, a student must memorize 10 poomse before being eligible to test for 1st Dan Black Belt.** True False

Answers:

1. False, 2. False, 3. False, 4. False, 5. True, 6. False, 7. True, 8. True, 9. True, 10. False, 11. False, 12. True, 13. True, 14. False, 15. True.

4TH GUP BLUE BELT
Belt of Patience

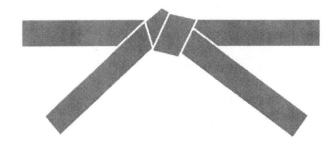

FOURTH (4TH) GUP – Blue Belt

1. Basic Fundamentals #1 – 28, *new 27 – 28 (pg 63 – 81)
2. Poom'se/Forms: (pg 84 – 95)
    a. Be prepared to perform all previous Forms
    b. Taegeuk Oh Chong (pg 94-95)
3. One Step Spar: #1 – 40, Advanced One Steps, (pg 104 – 116)
4. Free Style Sparring: (pg 117 – 121)
    a. Controlled Contact two 2 min. rounds
    b. Controlled Contact two 2 min. rounds (face, head & body attack with hands only)
5. Written/Oral Quiz – Subject: Sparring and Self-defense; The Sport of Taekwondo, (pg 104-120, 124-135)
6. Portfolio Check

Alternative Children's Curriculum

1. Basic Fundamentals #1 – 24, *new 21-24 (pg 63 – 79)
2. Poom'se/Forms: (pg 84 – 95)
    a. Taegeuk Sa Chong (pg 92-93)
    b. Taegeuk Oh Chong (pg 94-95)
3. One Step Spar: #1 – 40, advanced techniques, (pg 104 – 116)
4. Free Style Sparring: (pg 117 – 121)
5. Written/Oral Quiz – Subject: Sparring and Self-defense; The Sport of Taekwondo, (pg 104-120, 124-135)
6. Portfolio Check

ORAL QUIZ FOR 4TH GUP CANDIDATES

1. While sparring a fellow student, you notice that he is kicking and striking without much control and could actually hurt you, your response would be to ask him, "Would you please use a little more control?" True False

2. A combination is "a giyup and a punch". True False

3. According to our textbook there are 10 different types of sparring. True False

4. One Step Sparring does not help a student to be better at Free style sparring. True False

5. The basic difference between sparring and fighting is that in fighting there is an intention to hurt plus there is anger. True False

6. Continued practice in free style sparring is the key to preventing an injury to yourself and to your opponent. True False

7. A student does not need to have a fake if his technique is fast enough. True False

8. The foot is our first and most important weapon of the human body. True False

9. Our defensive system is the ability to parry away from and to block with our arms and hands. True False

10. The knee or leg block should only be used in a self-defense situation. True False

11. You should always look at the point where you are blocking. True False

12. Always look in the face of your opponent. True False

13. In order to strike high, you should fake low. True False

14. Free style sparring and tournament sparring are classified as the same. True False

15. Judo is a Japanese martial art. True False

Answers: 1. True, 2. False, 3. False, 4. False, 5. True, 6. True, 7. False, 8. False, 9. True, 10. True, 11. False, 12. False, 13. True, 14. False, 15. True.

REQUIREMENTS NEEDED TO GRADUATE THROUGH THE ADVANCED STAGES

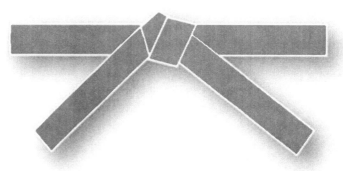

3rd GUP RED BELT
Belt of Energy

THIRD (3rd) GUP – Red Belt

1. Basic Fundamentals #1 – 28, (pg 63 – 81)

2. Poom'se/Forms: (pg 84 – 97)
   a. Be prepared to perform all previous Forms
   b. Taegeuk Yuk Chong (pg 96 – 97)

3. One Step Spar: #1 – 40, 40 advanced techniques (pg 104 – 116)

4. Free Style Sparring:
   Controlled Contact two 2 min. rounds (pg 117 – 121, 124-129,130)

5. Stamina Test: Pushups, Situps, 5 minutes run

6. Written/Oral Quiz – Subject: Vital and vulnerable areas of the human body; breaking; self-defense. (pg 135, 205-220)

7. Portfolio check

ADVANCED STAGE

CONGRATULATIONS!!! Upon being awarded a RED belt (3rd gup), you have now graduated to the Advanced Stage of training. During this stage you will prepare you for your Black Belt test.

It is extremely important that you attend special clinics, seminars hosted by your school or sponsored by the U.S. Chung Do Kwan Association, and additional class sessions whenever possible.

An important part of preparation for black belt is giving back. One way to do this is by learning how to teach and coach others. Attending the USCDKA NCIT (National Certified Instructors Training) Course will certify you to apply for an Instructors Degree after Black Belt and help you in obtaining your required Instructing Hours.

ORAL QUIZ FOR 3RD GUP CANDIDATES

1. According to our textbook there are six vulnerable targets in the chest area.   True   False

2. A vital area is an area on the human body where if struck with a hard blow could cause serious injury or death.   True   False

3. TaeKwonDo makes major joints into weapons.   True   False

4. The most practical stance in street defense is the forward square stance.   True   False

5. When breaking a board with a side chop, the entire edge of the hand is used, from the tip of the little finger down to the wrist.   True   False

6. It makes no difference how the boards are held as long as you strike in the middle.   True   False

7. According to our textbook, it takes approximately 40 pounds of pressure to break one 1" x 12" x 12" pine board.   True   False

8. Our textbook gives four classifications of demonstrations.   True   False

9. A student would have no problem breaking several concrete slabs on bare ground as long as he has the proper stance.   True   False

10. The author of our textbook estimates that it takes 250 pounds of pressure to break a red house brick.   True   False

11. The "Kukkiwon" is the administrative and research center of the World TaeKwonDo Federation.   True   False

12. Normally, a student must test ten times before being awarded the Black Belt.   True   False

13. Board holders must station themselves in a straddle stance before the strike is delivered.   True   False

14. There are six points of body balance.   True   False

15. A "Testing Cycle" is a student examination that is held monthly, bi-monthly or quarterly and evaluates a student under stressful situations.   True   False

Answers:
1. True, 2. True, 3. True, 4. False, 5. False, 6. False, 7. False, 8. True, 9. False, 10. True, 11. True, 12. True, 13. False, 14. False, 15. True.

SECOND (2ND) GUP – Brown Belt

Belt of Skill

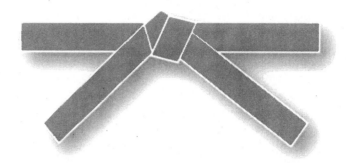

SECOND (2ND) GUP – Brown Belt

1. Basic Fundamentals #1 – 28, (pg 63-83)

2. Poomse / Forms

    a. Be prepared to perform all previous Forms, (pg 84-97)

    b. Taegeuk Chil Chong, (98-99)

3. One-Step Spar: #1 – 40, 50 Advanced Techniques, (pg 104-116)

4. Free Style Sparring, (pg 117-120, 123-135)

    a. Controlled contact: two, 2-minute rounds

    b. Technical Free Style Sparring (Advanced)

5. Stamina Test: Pushups, Sit-ups, 5 minute run

6. Written / Oral Quiz – Subject: Gup requirements; coaching, (pg 152-173)

7. Portfolio Check

Preparation Tips on your pathway to Black Belt
Black Belt should be within sight in your goal setting. Keeping your portfolio up to date, logging your Instructing Hours in your portfolio, and completing the requirements of participating in tournaments, seminars, and demonstrations should be a priority.

ORAL QUIZ FOR 2ND GUP CANDIDATES

1. One of the requirements for 9th Gup is to execute Taegeuk El Chong — True / False

2. To become a USCDK Green Belt, one must learn at least 20 one step spar techniques. — True / False

3. After being awarded a Blue Belt a USCDK student is then taught Taegeuk Oh Chong. — True / False

4. While coaching a beginner the most effective position for demonstrating a technique is along side of him/her. — True / False

5. When applying a hook kick during free style sparring, you should strike with the heel. — True / False

6. Continued practice and experience in free style sparring, teaches the student to "roll with the blow", therefore preventing serious injuries. — True / False

7. Poomse (forms) should only be practiced under the supervision of a Black Belt Instructor. — True / False

8. When in a self defense situation and the assailant has a weapon, it is imperative that you focus your attention on the assailants eyes. — True / False

9. Poomse is a training method in which a student learns to develop discipline. — True / False

10. According to our textbook there are two channels of the subconsciousness. — True / False

11. There are six ways that a specific kick can be applied. — True / False

12. The pressure points on the human body are approximately every six inches. — True / False

13. A pressure point is the accumulation of nerve endings. — True / False

14. Rape is the world's oldest social crime. — True / False

15. Name and reputation may pass away, but credentials last a lifetime. — True / False

Answers:
1. False, 2. True, 3. False, 4. True, 5. False, 6. True, 7. False, 8. True, 9. True, 10. False, 11. True, 12. True, 13. True, 14. True, 15. True

FIRST (1ST) GUP Brown Belt with Black Stripe

Belt of Competency

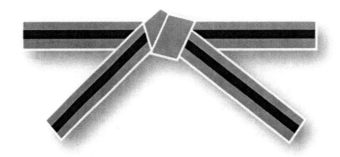

FIRST (1ST) GUP – Brown Belt with Black Strike through center

1. Basic Fundamentals #1 – 28, (pg 63-83)

2. Poomse / Forms

    a. Be prepared to perform all previous Forms, (pg 84-99)

    b. Taegeuk Pil Chong, (pg 100-101)

3. One-Step Spar: #1 – 40, 50 Advanced Techniques, (pg 104-116)

4. Free Style Sparring, (pg 117-120, 123-135)

    a. Controlled contact: two, 2-minute rounds

    b. Technical Free Style Sparring (Advanced)

5. Stamina Test: Pushups, Sit-ups, 5 minute run

6. Written / Oral Quiz – Subject: The art of instructing Taekwondo

7. USCDK Portfolio – Submit for first review

8. Brown Belt Term Paper: "What strengths has Taekwondo given to the physical and spiritual man within you?

NOTE: The final result for the 1st Gup examination will determine the time period of 3 to 9 months before you test for Black Belt.

ORAL QUIZ FOR 1ST GUP CANDIDATES

1. A person does not automatically become an Instructor after being awarded a Black Belt.   True   False

2. To qualify for the position as a USCDK Instructor, a student must first attend special seminars and training sessions prior to testing for 1st Dan.   True   False

3. A "special class" is a session when a specific item is taught during the entire time period.   True   False

4. An Associate Instructor has the authority to open his own school or club.   True   False

5. A Chief Instructor must hold the rank of at least 3rd Dan.   True   False

6. A student can become a Master after six years of training.   True   False

7. While teaching Poomse, the Instructor should remain in one position at all times so that he does not distract the students.   True   False

8. It is important for the Instructor to watch facial expressions in order to determine a change in a students temperment.   True   False

9. If an injury occurs during class, it would be wise for the Instructor to close the class and dismiss the students rapidly.   True   False

10. Body language is the "key" to reading the overall attitude of an adult class session.   True   False

11. An Instructor should never teach more than two "special class sessions" consecutively without having a Six Part Formal Class.   True   False

12. A Black Belt must register with the USCDK Headquarters every 2 years.   True   False

13. The author of our textbook gives a total of twelve rules on "how to win in forms and sparring" when entering a tournament.   True   False

14. A person must be a 4th Dan before qualifying for "International Referee Certification".   True   False

15. The jury at a tournament using WTF rules can "over-rule" all other officials.   True   False

Answers:
1. True, 2. True, 3. True, 4. False, 5. False, 6. True, 7. False, 8. True, 9. False, 10. True, 11. True, 12. False, 13. True, 14. False, 15. True

Black Belt

NOTE: Upon being certified, student will then receive the decorative USCDK Assoc. Black Belt with Gold Embroidery.

FIRST (1ST) DEGREE - Black Belt

1. Poom'se/Forms:
   a. All previous Forms (8)
   b. Da'lee Hyung El Chong
   c. Korya
2. Precision (touch) One-Step Spar, unlimited
   a. Technical Free Style Sparring; two rounds, 2 minutes
   b. Multiple sparring, two or more on one for 3 minutes
   c. Be prepared to defend yourself against a street weapon
4. Written/Oral Quiz -Subject: All Chapters in this Textbook plus material covered at Instructor's Course.
5. Black Belt Term Paper: 250 word essay - What philosophy do you have in your life and your TaeKwonDo future? It should contain "What the new rank of Black Belt means to you."
6. Breaking Technique: After getting advice and permission from your Instructor, you may perform any breaking technique that you have never done before.
7. Prerequisites:
   a. Must have attended a two-day or five-day seminar
   b. Must have accumulated no less than 25 hours of coaching or assistance to the Instructor
   c. Must have appeared before an appointed USCDK Black Belt Reviewing Board (Pre-Testing)
   d. Must have participated in no less than three exhibitions.
   e. Must have competed in or placed on an organizational committee of at least three tournaments.
   f. Must submit an official USCDK Portfolio, complete with all past TaeKwonDo activities and all your contributions to the success of your school and this association.

FIRST (1ST) DEGREE BLACK BELT (Confirmation/Certified)

1. Time period: Six months after last examination
2. Poom'se/Forms:
   a. All previous Forms
   b. Keum'Gong
3. Prerequisite: Written recommendation and report from Instructor concerning student's progress and contributions made since last examination.

WHAT IS A BLACK BELT?
A BLACK BELT IS A CHAMPION

First of all, let me explain the meaning of a Black Belt... "A Black Belt is a champion...a champion of his own weaknesses." EBS

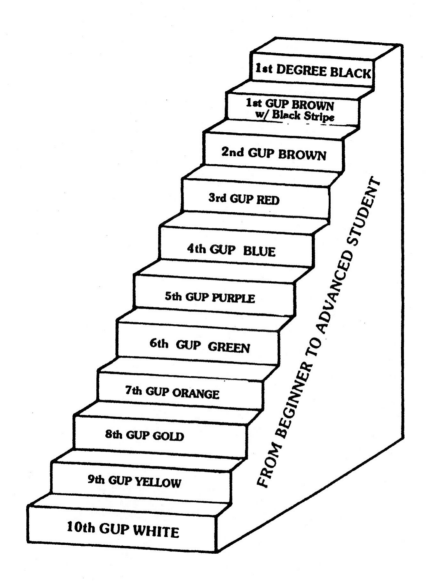

THIS WAY TO BLACK BELT

WOMEN IN TAE KWON DO

6

WOMEN IN TAEKWONDO

In the United States, TaeKwonDo (Korean Karate) is constantly climbing in popularity. In every community, city and state, hundreds and thousands of potential students and spectators come to see demonstrations, and tournament competition involving TaeKwonDo, an ancient martial art.

Of great interest to the public is the ever increasing number of women performing and practicing TaeKwonDo. With American women becoming more independent and conscious of their appearance today, they are turning to TaeKwonDo for protection (self-defense) and for physical fitness.

Some of the reasons there is such an increase of women practitioners of TaeKwonDo are as follows:

1. TaeKwonDo is more popular, increasing the number of women beginners.
2. TaeKwonDo is a very effective means of self-defense, drawing much interest in the training on the part of the intermediate female student.
3. TaeKwonDo is becoming a sport that adds confidence and self-esteem to the advanced student.
4. TaeKwonDo provides an excellent hobby and unlimited opportunities for the woman who wishes to develop a career when she reaches the Black Belt ranks.

The female student should not be regarded as a frail person whom no one can use much force on. If she wanted this image, she might have enrolled in ballet or yoga. Women students desire to be treated as equals to the men on the training floor. It takes a great deal for a woman to step on that training floor for the first time and she should be respected for it.

TaeKwonDo is the most exciting form of exercise a person could ever find. Because women are basically agile, the kicks and techniques can be transformed into a very beautiful and graceful art, developing poise and balance.

The male students strive for the finesse and beauty of form the female student exhibits, as the female student strives for the power so natural to the male student.

The female has more of the hormone estrogen, which produces a higher fat level, usually in the legs, hips, and thighs. Men have more of the hormone androgen, which affects certain bones. Specifically, the male shoulders are wider. If you take the prototype of male and female and stand them next to each other, the female will be wider in the pelvic area (generally) and the male wider in the shoulder area.

The result of this comparison is a difference in the center of gravity. A woman basketball player usually cannot execute a jump shot the same way a man can. Men can hang in the air, women cannot. A woman trying to execute a jump kick is anchored down by a lower center of gravity.

There is very little difference in men and women as far as endurance is concerned. It is primarily a strength due to hormonal differences. Through continuous practice, the female student will tone her muscles, (not build them) and learn to shift body weight in order to "focus power" in an effective way.

Women are a great asset to any school. Their agility can be a great encouragement to all beginners and with continued support from other women students and the intructor, they can come to accomplish the same feats the male students can and in some cases with more poise, grace and determination.

"Little Women" in action.

WOMEN'S PROGRESS IN A MALE DOMINATED SPORT

Thinking back on how far TaeKwonDo has come, I can remember in 1970 competing in some of the largest tournaments in the United States. At one particular tournament in Ohio there were almost 500 competitors. The women's division consisted of 8. Back in those days, all women were in one division, white to brown (there were no Black Belt women around) regardless of rank, age or size. There were several times the lower ranking women could win the event because of determination on her part and over confidence on the part of her opponent. I recall how even during the infant stages of Women in TaeKwonDo, spectators would be in awe as they watched the drive, ambition and competitive spirit the women's division displayed in comparison to other divisions. There was never any glory (other than another trophy or perhaps her name in the club newsletter), but the female TaeKwonDo practitioner has continued to perserve taking each step as a personal challenge in this male dominated sport.

In 1978 I attended the Pre-World TaeKwonDo Championships in Seoul, Korea at the invitation of WTF President Un Yong Kim. This was to be the first time women were to be included in international TaeKwonDo competition. The men's competition was fabulous as each competitor displayed talent, integrity, respect and confidence. However, there was little to be proud of as the womens teams competed. The women were not prepared, nor were they trained properly for international competition. I don't believe it was the female competitors fault, but rather people in places of authority not looking at the opportunity seriously. Nevertheless the lack of preparation and experience showed.

Today, women are still battling to have the same opportunities as men. In my experience, I've never seen a dedicated female TaeKwonDo practitioner who viewed herself as a woman while training, rather she views herself as an artist with equal talents and ability. On the training floor there should never be a "battle of the sexes". TaeKwonDo is a unique sport because size, age nor sex restrict the practitioner from participating. I remember back in the late 70's attending an International Referee Seminar where I was the first woman to pass the International Referee exam. A Korean Master from another country asked me if I would kick for him because he had never witnessed a female practicing TaeKwonDo. He was amazed that there was no difference in my kicks and his! I was just as surprised at his ignorance of women in TaeKwonDo as he was to the potential.

Well, I'm convinced the female athletes of tennis, gymnastics and volleyball had similar experiences and I predict female TaeKwonDo athletes will some day soon have the same respect and admiration of those athletes of other sports.

We are off to a good start. Today, women in international competition are in great demand as they train hard and the general public looks at the determination of this new generation of female TaeKwonDo athletes. Keep your eyes on the women - you won't be disappointed.

Brenda J. Sell
5th Degree Kukkiwon Black Belt

SELF DEFENSE FOR WOMEN

Throughout the centuries, women have always been labeled the "weaker sex." To some this term is offensive, to others it simply means the female population is more delicate and complex. However you view it, it cannot be argued that women are in need of self protection more than the male population. In this chapter we intend to present thorough research and attention to this area. Every individual is worth defending. God has a special plan for each one of us, and it is up to us to find it. Our next subject will be RAPE and how to avoid and/or cope with the situation, but first let us begin with a few basics.

There are 13 basic weapons on each side of the body: the fist, the back of the fist, and edge of the fist, the edge of the hand, the ridge of the hand, the heel of the hand, the fingers, the elbow, the knee, the top of the foot, the ball of the foot, the edge of the foot and the heel. (See page 12.) With proper training, all of these joints may be turned into weapons. Practice and conditioning are imperative to the serious student.

The fist is the most common weapon used. Improper delivery could cause serious injury. At this time it would be wise to turn to page 14 for instructions of how to make a proper fist.

Body balance is of the utmost importance in self defense and martial arts in general. There are actually 8 points of body balance. If you were to stand with both feet together, there are only 8 ways in which you could fall. They would be the same as the 8 points on a compass.

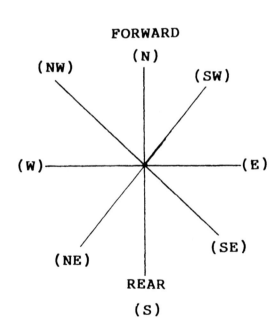

Proper foot positioning corresponds with body balance. During this chapter you will be directed to the fighting stance as your primary defense position. By stepping backwards into a fighting stance you have eliminated 6 of the 8 off balance positions. Incredible? Not really, just scientific. It must be understand that TaeKwonDo is a science, as well as an art.

BASIC HAND TECHNIQUES AND THE BASIC VITAL AREAS

BACK FIST: temple, bridge of nose, base of nose
FOUR KNUCKLE PUNCH: windpipe
STRAIGHT PUNCH: bridge of nose, base of nose, solar plexus
HAMMER BLOW: bridge of nose, base of nose, temple, cerebellum, groin
TWO FINGER SPEAR: eyes
KNIFE HAND: base of nose, throat, collar bone, windpipe

BACK FIST

FOUR KNUCKLE PUNCH

STRAIGHT PUNCH

HAMMER BLOW

TWO FINGER SPEAR

KNIFE HAND

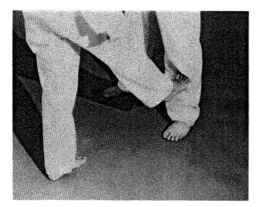
Front Kick
(to the shins)

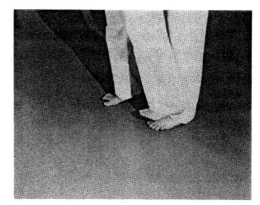
Heel of the Foot
(insteps)

FOOT TECHNIQUES

The legs are naturally longer and stronger than the arms. The feet are naturally stronger than the hands. Practice kicking techniques from the knee instead of straight legged. Learn to focus into the vital areas and your techniques will be more effective through "focused power."

Round Kick
(solar plexus)

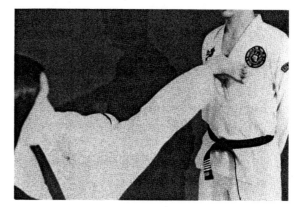
Side Kick
(chest)

APPLY COMMON SENSE

1. Be prepared.

2. Avoid dangerous situations
    a. Plan the shortest distance between two places.
    b. Choose a well lighted route.

3. RUN as soon as you can.

4. You must react immediately to have the advantage. The element of surprise is in your favor. If you must fight, memorize the following rules:

A. Do not execute any technique that is new, or that is not comfortable to you on an attacker.

B. You must have quick, automatic reflexes and responses.

C. Foot positioning is important for balance and effective techniques.

D. Always keep the momentum going in the same direction as your opponent is moving and apply your techniques in that same direction.

THE FUNDAMENTALS OF FOCUSING A TECHNIQUE

1. Use a technique which feels most natural to you.

2. Use a technique adaptable to circumstances (weather, season, environment.)

3. Have alternatives and variations prepared in case the attacker changes positions.

4. Focus your technique on a specific area (target). Correct technique must be used to maximize the effect to a vulnerable area.

5. Prepare yourself to have several follow-up techniques in case the main striking technique is not effective.

6. POWER. - All of the above are ineffective unless there is power. The force must be sufficient to reduce any further attack.

Women Can Fight Back!

Grandmaster Brenda Sell demonstrates a controlled round kick to Master Bernie Fritts

STRATEGIES FOR SELF DEFENSE

First of all, know your enemy. He can become a very violent person. He expects you to be frightened and weak. His motive is to degrade you and possibly brutalize you.

Be prepared to move out of his way fast!! The element of surprise is in your favor. Make noises, scream, break windows. Low, fast kicks to the shins or hard, powerful blows to the vital areas of the body will aid you in warding off your opponent.

Attacker attempts to grab you and has no weapon:
Goal: Scare him off or stun him so you can escape.

You must react immediately to have any advantage. Study the breaking of holds in this chapter and apply whichever is the most suitable. Distract him by screaming or kicking. If you struggle ineffectively, this may only antagonize him and cause him to apply more force.

The majority of women who have successfully thwarted an attack have used noise exclusively. Make as much noise anyway you are able. Knock things over, break windows, yell, do anything to attract attention. When you yell, make sure you say POLICE or HELP, so if someone does hear you, they may respond themselves or telephone the police for you.

The Gi-yup or yell plays a very important part in formal TaeKwonDo training, and the benefits received from these class sessions can definitely be of use in a dangerous situation. If the gi-yup is applied properly, the yell comes from the pit of the stomach, not the throat. The gi-yup, when applied properly, will result in the following:

a. You will obtain more power.
b. You may possibly startle your opponent or scare him.
c. You may cause the attacker to hesitate.
d. You will reduce the tension in your own body.
e. Decrease your own awareness of pain.

ARM GRAB

Twist wrist toward thumb & finger opening.

Jerk away hard & fast

Strike to throat

A.

B.

C.

D.

A. Attack
B. Place your right thumb at assailants center knuckle, left hand under his elbow.
C. Step back with the right foot; twist the arm applying a downward pressure on the elbow, pulling upward on the hand.
D. Front snap kick to the solar plexus or face.

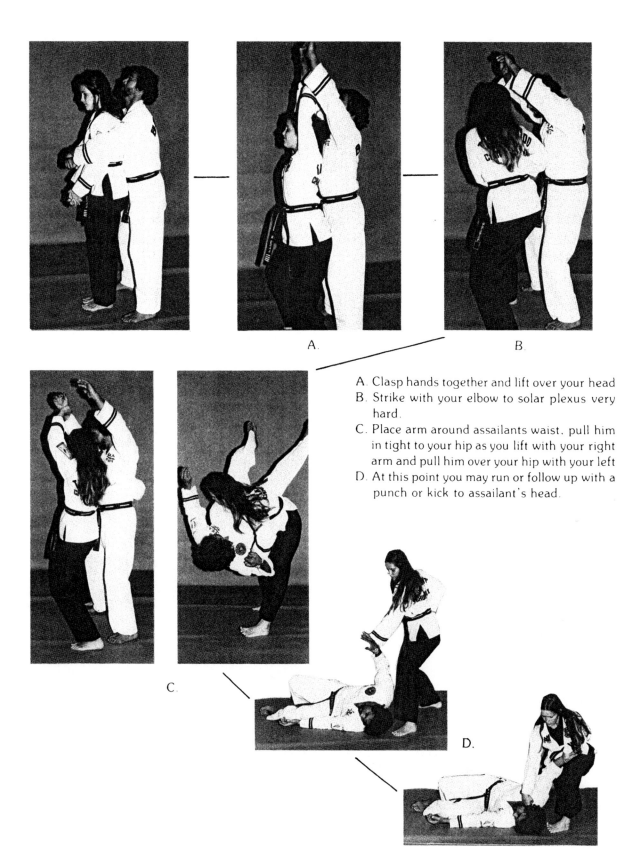

A. Clasp hands together and lift over your head
B. Strike with your elbow to solar plexus very hard.
C. Place arm around assailants waist. pull him in tight to your hip as you lift with your right arm and pull him over your hip with your left
D. At this point you may run or follow up with a punch or kick to assailant's head.

TWO ASSAILANTS

A. When being held by one assailant, lean backwards lift both feet off the ground.

B. Bend your knees, cup both your hands together.

C. Kick #2 assailant with both feet as hard as you can.

C. Bend your knees, cup both your hands together.

D. Lift both arms over your head.

E. Elbow to solar plexus and run away.

A. Attack

B. Pull little fingers of assailant back as far as possible, until he release the hold.

C. Back kick to groin.

A. Attack

B. Pull assailant #1 into you, side kick.

C. Round kick to the temple of assailant #2.

PRECAUTIONS AT HOME

1. Have a deadbolt lock put on your door, (these cannot be jimmied.)

2. Place a long stick or broom handle in the track of the sliding glass door.

3. A chain lock, or peep hole will aid you to check the identity of visitors before allowing them to enter.

4. When returning home, have your keys ready before you get to your door.

5. If you live alone, list fake house mates on your mailbox.

6. Do not allow a stranger to enter your home to use your telephone. Make the call for him.

7. When you are not at home keep the drapes closed, and used timed lights.

8. If when you return home, the doors or windows have been forced or broken, go to a neighbors house and call the police. Do not enter alone!!

9. Report suspicious persons, vehicles, or incidents to the police.

10. Change the locks when moving into a new home.

PRECAUTIONS IN YOUR CAR

1. Carry your keys in your hand when approaching your car.

2. Park your car in a well lit area.

3. When shopping, have large packages delivered to your home.

4. Keep your car doors locked at all times.

5. Before getting into your car, look into the back seat, and on the floors.

6. Don't give a ride to a stranger.

7. Don't let the gas tank get below ¼ full.

8. Keep your car in good working order and have it checked frequently.

9. If you are being followed, do not drive home. Drive to the police station, and write down the license plate number of the car.

10. If you are threatened and cannot move to get away, use the horn to draw attention.

PRECAUTIONS ON THE STREET

1. If you are able to maneuver the site of a potential confrontation, choose an even surface with plenty of space for yourself.

2. Always keep your arms up and ready to deflect any grab or punch, but do not venture close enough to punch at him. If you have no room to step back, strike to his throat.

3. Stay back and kick instead of punching. Kick from your knee instead of straight legged.

4. Keep him at bay by a series of low, rapid kicks aimed at his knees.

5. If someone grabs your wrist, use leverage to pry up against his thumb. React quickly before he can get a proper grip.

6. If you can't break his hold, immediately counterattack with kicks before he expects it.

7. Make all the noise you can. Break someone's window to attract attention. Yell "Police!" or "Help!!".

8. If someone grabs you from behind, do your best to stay on your feet. You can even lean against him to maintain your balance.

9. If he attempts to choke you with his forearm from behind, turn your throat into the crook of his elbow.

10. If he attempts to choke you with his hands, wrench his little fingers backward and dislocate them.

11. When held from behind, bring your heel down over his kneecap, scrape down his shin and slam into his instep.

12. Immediately kick up again into his knee and repeat everything rapidly until he lets go of you.

13. If he grabs your wrists, remember the thumbs are the weakest part of your attackers grip. Pull your arms toward his thumbs to break away.

14. Your resistance to an attack will generally stimulate your opponent. Cooperate until you can counter attack into a vital area effectively.

15. If you think someone is following you, turn around and look. Know your opponent and anticipate his moves.

PURSE SNATCHING

HAIR GRASP

A. Attack

B. Clasp your hands together at his wrist.

C. Apply downward pressure

D. Front kick to the throat.

Crescent kick to head

Push head into wall.

Be alert and take advantage of every opportunity to strike or for anything that may be used as a weapon.

RAPE

The World's Oldest Social Crime

RAPE is the oldest crime, and women are it's natural victims. Rape is a different kind of crime; it does not net the offender any money or goods. It is a crime of violence. Rape is not even primarily a sexual act.

According to Webster, rape is "the illicit carnal knowledge of a woman without her consent." Down through history there have been countless rapes by individuals and mass rapes by invading armies. The most recent was in 1972 when 20,000 women were brutally raped by West Pakistani soldiers. It was part of their military strategy.

While murder and robbery are on the decline, the number of rapes raised 93% in the past decade! Like murder, rape is a hostile act that is most likely to occur between two people who are acquainted or live in the same neighborhood. Fortunately, most rapists do not kill their victims after they have brutalized and disgraced them.

There are approximately 55,000 rapes reported a year - one every ten minutes. For every 1,000 rapes reported, 900 are not reported. Of those 1,000 rapes reported, arrests are made in 300 cases and 33 go to trial. Out of those, only 3 are convicted. College students are prime victims. The rise of rapes on campuses is almost too great to even estimate. The youngest rape victim ever reported was a 15 month old baby, and the oldest was a 92 year old woman.

All women are in danger - even you. <u>Self defense begins in your head</u>. You must feel you are worth defending. As a woman, you can and must protect yourself. All women must confront the feelings of fear, weakness, and inadequacy. It is crucial that you learn to be strong, alert and ready. Every time you imagine an emergency or dangerous situation you are preparing. Instead of fearing future harm, think about it, and consider calmly each possibility. Such a consciousness will keep you alive, in control of yourself, and in control of situations you find yourself in.

MYTHS ABOUT RAPE

"...many people believe the typical rapist is a complete stranger." This is usually not true. A large percentage of rapists are known to the victim, either casual friends, or maybe even a relative. Many rapists live in the same neighborhood as their victims. Women must be aware that they cannot trust all the men with whom they are acquainted.

"...a rapist is a sexually unfulfilled man carried away by an uncontrollable desire." This is one of the more popular myths. The fact is that about 50-60% of the rapes committed by single men are planned. Many of the men are married and lead normal sexual lives at home.

"...all rapists are 'pathologically sick' and 'perverted' men." Sex is *not* the motivating factor in most rapes...it is merely a way of expressing violence and rage. According to recent studies, most men convicted of rape have normal sexual personalities. They usually differ only in that they have a greater tendency to express violence and rage.

"...most rapes occur in dark back alleys." Over one third of the rapes reported are committed by a man who forces his way into the victims home. Over one half of all these rapes committed occur in a residence.

"...black men rape white women whenever possible." In most rapes, (85%-95%) the man and woman are of the same race. In **fact**, white men attack black women with more frequency than black men attack white women.

"...rape is impossible without the consent of the woman." Or, "...women actually enjoy being raped." How absurd!!! The woman may be knocked unconscious, or threatened with her family's lives, or even her own life, or she may simply be in shock, or overpowered. Men are physically stronger than women. There have been instances when women trained in self-defense have been overpowered and raped. The element of surprise is the key for a woman who is trying to defend herself. If that key factor is gone, her chances of escape are minimal. As for her actually enjoying it, how could anyone enjoy sex with someone they are not attracted to or with whom they are forced to participate?

"IT COULD NEVER HAPPEN TO ME..."

"IF HE HAS A WEAPON, SHOULD I SUBMIT???"

"COULD I HURT HIM OR COULD HE HURT ME MORE???"

"BUT WHAT IF SOMEONE DOES ATTACK ME???"

You don't have to become a victim. AVOID rape, make yourself S.A.F.E.

S. - Secure yourself.
A. - Avoid trouble.
F. - Flee if possible
E. - Entertain him, if necessary

Secure yourself by keeping your doors locked while driving, leaving the car, and at home. Have your keys ready when you arrive at the door of your home. Be ready!

Avoid trouble by not walking on dark, poorly lit streets. Stay away from alleys and bushes where someone could be hiding. Carry your purse tightly under your arm, not dangling. Walk home in pairs or groups, check the back seat of your car before getting in, use your intuitions of danger. If you feel a man is eager to get you off alone, see if he's as interested in you when you suggest that another friend or couple come along. Stay alert and be wary of people near by.

Flee if possible. Don't wear high heel shoes, wear shoes you can easily run in.

Entertain him, if necessary. Try to gain his confidence. If you can, stay calm, try delaying tactics or try talking.

FIGHTING should be a last resort. This means no holds barred. The action must be decisive. Struggling ineffectively may only excite the attacker. Gouging at eyes with your fingers, or a vicious kick to the groin may be necessary, but you must learn to do it right, you may NEVER get a second chance.

REPORTING TO THE POLICE

If you have been threatened or attacked, try to remain calm and observe the characteristics of the assailant. Try to memorize the following and record on paper as soon as possible.

1. Sex
2. Age
3. Skin color
4. Hair color & style
5. Eye color and shape
6. Teeth
7. Shape of nose
8. Height
9. Weight
10. Scars, marks, tatoos
11. Clothing
12. Mustache or beard
13. Body build
14. Voice, speech characteristics

Although police procedures vary from one jurisdiction to another, the following sequence of steps could be expected in most criminal sexual conduct cases:

1. If an assault occurs, the victim should contact the police as soon as possible after the attack. The officers must be advised of the physical description of the attacker, his last known location and the direction and method of his escape. This information will be broadcast to all area police agencies, who can then begin a search for the suspect while a car is being sent to meet with the victim.

2. While awaiting the arrival of the police, a victim should never change clothing or bathe. Valuable evidence, such as hairs and body fluid stains, may be destroyed. Do not disturb the scene of the crime. This will also be processed for physical evidence.

3. When the first officers arrive, the victim will relate the details of the incident to them. It is their responsibility to complete the original report of the crime.

4. Generally, a detective will be contacted to: (1) process the scene for physical evidence, (2) conduct an in-depth interview with the victim or (3) both of the above. Most police agencies have female detectives to interview the victim if she would feel more comfortable discussing the incident with a woman. The victim should be prepared to answer a great many personal and often embarrassing questions. This cannot be avoided. To prosecute a criminal case, it is necessary that the exact acts involved be clearly defined.

5. Often before the in-depth interview is conducted, the victim will be transported to the hospital for an examination specifically directed to recovering physical evidence. If injuries have occured which are visible, such as a black eye or scratches, cuts, and bruises, these will be photographed. Generally, the victims clothing will also be collected by police at this time to be held as evidence. (Later the clothing will be examined for semen stains, hairs, fibers and damage).

6. The hospital or the police will then contact a caseworker from the Assault Crisis Center is such an agency is available in their area. This is very helpful for the victim. The caseworker stays with the victim from that point onward and is able to provide counseling or other assistance. This relationship is maintained not only that day, but until the trial itself is completed, often even months later.

7. If the suspect is as yet unidentified, the victim will be asked to assist in various ways with the investigation. She may be asked to view photos of potential suspects, make a composite drawing of the suspect or make further statements concerning the events surrounding the attack.

8. If the suspect is in custody, the next step is to meet with the prosecutor. It is his responsibility to authorize a request for a ciminal warrant charging the defendant with the specific crime. In most instances, the prosecutor will want to hear the details of the case directly from the victim rather than from a police report. This is important for several reasons: (1) It gives the prosecutor an opportunity to evaluate the credibility of the victim. (2) It allows an opportunity for the victim and prosecutor to establish a rapport, which is very important later during the court proceedings. (3) It forces the victim to relate the story again. Although this may be difficult, she will have to relate the details of the crime in its entirety to complete strangers in the courtroom, and this gives her another occasion during which she can "practice".

9. If the warrant is authorized, the victim will appear before a judge, who will also question her as to the details, and sign the warrant (the legal document formally causing the defendant to be brought before the court to answer a specific charge.)

10. The next step is the preliminary examination. This is a hearing, not a trial, to which the defendant is entitled. At this exam, the State must show: (1) That a crime was committed, and (2) That there is probable cause to believe that the defendant committed the crime. In all cases the victim will testify to the acts committed against her, and must be sufficiently specific to satisfy the requirements of the law. If she is able, she will also identify the defendant, who will be present in the courtroom. If she cannot identify the defendant, other witnesses will be produced to tie this defendant to the crime.

11. After the examination, the defendant will be bound over to Circuit Court for trial (if the proof was sufficient; if not, the case is dismissed after the examination). In Circuit Court, a trial will be held from one to six months later. During this trial, the State must prove, "beyond a reasonable doubt," that the defendant is guilty. The victim will again relate all the details of the incident and will again be subjected to cross-examination by the defendant's attorney.

12. If the defendant is found guilty, he will be sentenced by the court.

MEDICAL AID

A woman who has been raped needs immediate medical attention. Not only for external injuries but also possible internal injuries. If there is even a slight chance the victim will press charges against the assailant, she must not bathe or even change clothes before going for a medical examination.

To establish that rape took place, there must be legal proof of penetration. This means a pelvic exam within 72 hours after the assault. The doctor will check for the presence of semen on the victim's body or clothing to be used for an analysis to determine the blood type of the rapist.

The doctor will write down on a police report form any signs of cuts, bruises, abrasions or any other signs which might verify abuse.

The doctor should discuss the possibility of VD as a result of the attack. A follow-up check should be made within six weeks of the rape, when VD can be detected. After the VD test the victim can request the bill be sent to the County Health Department. The Health Department will pay for the test and treatment.

The doctor should also discuss the possibility of pregnancy and the alternatives available.

The rape victim should ask for a complete explanation of any medication prescribed for her. Especially with respect to DES, a drug also known as "the morning after pill." The victim should be made aware of the many known side effects linked to this pill.

15 BASIC RULES FOR SELF-DEFENSE

1. Do not use any technique on an attacker that is not comfortable to you. Don't try anything new on an attacker!

2. You must have quick, automatic reflexes and responses.

3. Foot positioning is important for balance and effective technique.

4. Always keep momentum going in the same direction that the opponent is moving and apply techniques in that same direction.

5. Be able to use hands, feet and throwing techniques equally.

6. When an opponent is down, try using kicks instead of bending over to deliver a hand technique.

7. Use your body as a weapon and utilize any available weapons: keys, pens, pencils, a comb, a can, a piece of glass, your shoes, even your purse.

8. Keep your eyes in the chest-waist area of your opponent, unless he has a weapon. By keeping your eye contact in this area you will be able to detect any moves he makes with his hands or feet before he makes them.

9. Keep hitting your attacker until you have reduced his capacity to follow you -- then RUN!!

10. If you think someone is following you, turn around and look. Don't be taken by surprise.

11. If you are confronted with a potential attacker, immediately step into an "on guard" position, such as the fighting stance described in this manual.

12. Quickly look for an escape route and look for anything that you may use for a weapon, if necessary.

13. Avoid dangerous situations:
    1. Plan the shortest distance between two places when travelling.
    2. Choose a well lighted route.
    3. When riding or driving in a car, keep all of the doors locked at all times, even if only travelling a short distance.

14. Above all DON'T PANIC.

15. When circumstances permit, RUN...MAKE NOISE...KNOCK THINGS OVER... ATTRACT ATTENTION...YELL POLICE, OR HELP, SO THAT ANYONE WHO MIGHT HEAR YOU KNOWS YOU ARE IN TROUBLE.

THE ART OF DEMONSTRATING

7

"The weakest point of any practical object is in the center."

"Practicing common sense by eliminating the impossible, a student in TaeKwonDo can break any practical object when concentrating on a focused point and shifting the proper amount of body weight at the maximum point of speed during the application of any technique."

The Author

WHAT IS A TAE KWON DO/KARATE DEMONSTRATION?

Also referred to as an exhibition, such a performance when properly organized and professionally executed has three primary objectives:

#1. It offers an instructor, as well as his students, an opportunity to display their skills and talents to the general public.

#2. It also gives the dedicated Black Belt Instructor an opportunity to "clean up" the image of TaeKwonDo and dispell many myths and rumors common among the non practitioner.

#3. Finally, it is a unique opportunity for the instructor and his students to promote their particular style and school in the search for potential students.

Even though it is not an everyday practice to break boards, bricks or concrete slabs during class sessions, it is very possible while performing in a demo, for each student to gain more confidence while assisting the instructor as they break boards and concrete with their bare hands and feet. Naturally, they must listen to the coaching of the Black Belt in charge before the students attempts these breaks.

It is the showmanship and professionalism of the Black Belt Instructor which determines the success or failure of the demonstration. With dedicated practice and experience, a karate demonstration can be extremely entertaining and educational to the general public.

The fact is that there are some individuals who thrive on public exposure and become very arrogant even to the extent of giving the impression of being an "egoist." It is very unfortunate, but in every profession and all walks of life, we must accept the fact that these people exist. A professional instructor who has geared his life toward the principles of the martial arts would not be found associating with this type of person.

The author refers to his performances as a "demonstration in the art and science of TaeKwonDo Korean Karate." He stresses that the "art" is: 1) the ability to perform "poom'se," (translated as the forms or patterns of defensive movement") and 2) the ability of "striking out with the hands and feet as hard and as fast as possible but stopping at the point of contact, as soon as flesh meets flesh." (Here he is referring to the mastery of One Step Sparring, which is indeed one of the most impressive demonstrations in physical and mental control ever executed by one human being upon another.) Then he explains the "science" of TaeKwonDo as "the ability to strike through one, two, three and even four inches of wood, solid concrete and thick house bricks with one blow of the hand or foot." He says that this is a simple science of shifting body weight at the point of contact or the center of any practical object.

Now let us analyze the "scientific part" of the demo a little further. He says that the "weakest point of any practical object is in the center." What can be considered a practical object? Certainly not a 2 x 4" of any length, a concrete block, an iron rod, or a brick wall. Such objects are only broken in the movies. The true martial artist must set a code of ethics, which can be tranlated into "the science as a moral code." 1) Never attempt to break anything that one would feel is impossible to break. 2) Never attempt to break anything that would be a degradation to the art. 3) Never attempt to break anything that may be a risk of possible injury. 4) Never attempt to break anything that would reflect "arrogance." 5) Never consume alcohol prior to attempting a break.

Since we have already emphasized the importance of shifting body weight, it becomes obvious that the more body weight one has to shift, the more "practical" material he would be able to break. The author has estimated that it would take approximately eighty pounds of pressure to break one inch of wood cut in the dimensions of 12" x 12". Therefore, if a person, let us say a junior grade student, weighs only 60 to 80 pounds, it would be very difficult for him to break a board equal to that size. It would be wise for the instructor to cut the board in half "width-wise" to make it easier for his student to complete the break. A student must not consider "breaking" until he has obtained the ability to formulate the following combinations: speed (SP), body weight (BW), concentration (C) and focus (F):

$$SP \times BW + C + F = POWER$$

It is the instructor's responsibility to encourage the student to start his breaking experiences using "easy to break" material until he has developed the skill of focusing his blow dead center on the material he plans to break.

The instructor should always be well aware of the students ability in breaking and never assign a student to break any material that he is not sure the student can break.

RULES TO REMEMBER BEFORE BREAKING WOOD

#1. Pine board has been the most popular wood in performing a successful break. Make sure that the grain is no less than ¼" apart. Elm, maple and oak boards have grain very close together and this can make it very difficult to break. Remember that a sensible break can only be done with the grain, not against it. When performing a demonstration, the author explains, as he holds up a board to the spectators, "Even King Kong could not break this board cross-grain, and even if you lay this board against a brick wall and hit it with an ax cross-grain, it will still break with the grain." Naturally he is holding a board 12 inches wide by 10 inches long when he says his now famous statement.

#2. The most important part in setting up for a break, is selecting not only the material, but also the board holders. They should be experienced enough to know exactly how to hold the boards.

#3. When selecting your wood, be sure to purchase well dried pine boards. An important rule to follow when storing any kind of demo material is to keep it high and never store in areas where moisture exists.

#4. The wood boards can be purchased in any lengths and you will find that your material will be less expensive if you do the cutting of each demo board. The author considers a 1" x12" x 12" to be a standard measurement for "official use," such as competition and perhaps for examination for higher rank, but he recommends that the average demo board be cut 12 inches wide by 9 or 10 inches long. White pine is the most commonly used wood material.

#5. It is very wise for the instructor to personally check all demo material just prior to the scheduled performance to prevent an embarrassing accidental break. Never purchase a board that has the heart of the grain running through the middle. When dried, the heart of the wood becomes very weak and the board can be broken even with the slightest touch.

#6. It would be foolish to glue the boards together or have them held by some mechanical device.

#7. When breaking more than one board, be sure that the grain of each board is running in the same direction. Take precautions to avoid wide air pockets between each board and never attempt to break boards that have been glued together. The boards must have room to expand or slide against one another if they are to be successfully broken. The restriction of the glue would cause a substantial increase in the strength of each board.

#8. In rule #2, we have emphasized the importance in properly holding the boards. The author wishes to discourage anyone from attempting to break boards that are held by mechanical devices such as vices, clamps or ones that are nailed to any type of platform. The effect would be similar to that of gluing each board as mentioned in rule #6. The restriction of movement or expansion will cause each board to increase its strength. The author explains that there is a unique principle behind having humans hold the boards: "The arms of the board holders will react as a slight cushion and assist in reducing the risk of pain or serious injury, especially if one should experience an unsuccessful break." At this point the author also wishes to discourage the use of the non student or spectator as the board holders, primarily for liability reasons, but also to insure that the boards will be held properly by well trained members of the demonstration team.

UNBELIEVABLE HIDDEN POWER

One of my favorite breaking techniques is four inches of wood with a round kick. This breaking technique would be equivalent to a 38 caliber pistol shot at point blank range into the human body. Recently I applied this theory by shooting a 38 caliber pistol point blank into four inches of wood. It was to my surprise that the bullet (slug) stopped its penetrating power at the crust of the third board. Therefore, theorectically speaking, "the round kick, when delivered by an expert, could very possibly have TWICE the impact of a 38 caliber pistol shot at point blank range into the human body."

It is a fact that the majority of martial artists go through brief stages of "egotism," normally at the very beginning of the training. Fortunately, we survive and soon realize such foolishness can become very harmful not only to our bodies but also in the development of a strong character. I learned to respect and appreciate the hidden powers of TaeKwonDo very early in my training. The key to learning the effectiveness of this hidden power that every person has, is to concentrate and practice very hard to focus with full and controlled power.

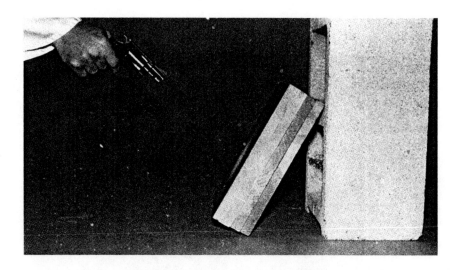

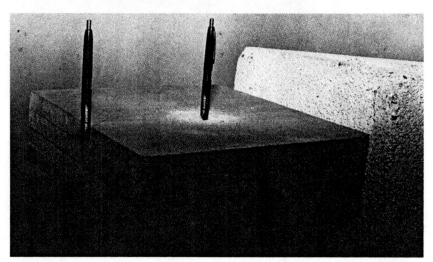

Unbelievable Hidden Power (cont.)

Each person creates a barrier that restricts him from going beyond his own expectations. Through the training of an authentic martial art system, a person can extend or even eliminate this barrier which keeps him from doing things that he normally would feel he couldn't do. To simplify this message, we can call this "the strengthening of one's confidence."

When performing in a demonstration or exercising one's skills in a martial art such as TaeKwonDo or Karate, the danger becomes very evident when a person becomes over confident and dares to trespass his "human limitations". The result of such foolish action can be broken skin, bruised and battered muscles and cracked or broken bones.

CLASSIFICATION OF A TKD/KARATE DEMONSTRATION

Here are the various types of demonstrations that the author and his students have performed during the past eighteen years.

Let us start with the most difficult demo, referred to as the "non-captive audience" and rated as a Class D Demo. This is a demonstration in which performers are exposed to the public, such as at a fairground with plenty of walk-by traffic and perhaps some hecklers.

Classification C is a demo performed before a group of young people, primarily aged six to fourteen. The advantage of this type of demo is that it has a captive audience, meaning the performers are inside a building with no other activities to distract either the spectators or the students. It is recommended that the instructor warn the youngsters not to attempt to practice what they see unless properly trained. He should also emphasize the risk of injury if any of them try to break a piece of wood or brick without conditioning themselves both physically and mentally.

Classification B is a demo performed before a group of adults within a building with a captive audience but out of the local area of the school being represented. Here the instructor has the challenge of presenting the art as well as he possibly can and, in an effort to clean up the misconceptions that many people have concerning karate in general. He must watch himself and his students very carefully so as not to give a poor representation. It is not absolutely necessary, but would be impressive and helpful to the art and the school for the instructor to hand out information pamphlets at his demo. At this type of demo, a pamphlet with easy to read, general information would assist him in his goal, which is simply to promote the art.

Classification A should be the most exciting and important demo for any school. The site should be within easy driving distance of the school and the audience should consist of youngsters, teens and adults of all ages. The audience should range from 100 to 500 or more and the primary objective would be to promote the art and the school searching for potential students.

RULES TO REMEMBER BEFORE BREAKING CONCRETE

#1. There are several types of concrete slabs ranging from one inch to six inches in thickness. First there is finely ground pressed concrete. Finely ground pressed and baked concrete (known as fire wall brick) is used primarily in the construction of large ovens. It would be wise to avoid this type of material. Second is coarsely ground pressed concrete. Coarsely ground, pressed and sprayed with a hardener, this material should be used only when there is no other available because it is much harder than the non-glued type and hardens with age, making it unpredictable at times. Third is the material most commonly used for impressive concrete breaks. It is not actually concrete but a mixture of coarse cinder gravel and cement powder. But let us not underestimate this material. It indeed takes a well focused blow to successfully break several slabs when stacked upon one another and the audience loves it. The average measurements of this type of slab is seven inches wide by fourteen inches long and, depending on the instructor's preference, one or two inches thick.

#2. Never allow a student with less than three months training to become involved with this type of "heavy breaking." One must condition his arms, wrists, and hands before attempting to break concrete, plus he must have the confidence and trust in his instructor before the break will be successful. The slightest doubt or hesitation could cause serious injury to his hand or wrist. Naturally, his ability to focus his body movement and the downward striking action of the hand must be considered before allowing him to attempt one of karate's most impressive breaking techniques.

#3. Using the proper stansion blocks is vitally important when setting up for this type of break. The most commonly used are cement blocks standing upright.

#4. The concrete break should be at the end of a demo, since the concrete and cinder does "splatter" when struck with a hard blow, meaning that the demonstration area should be swept in order to prevent injuries to bare feet during the remaining part of the demo. It may also be necessary to place the stansion blocks on a larger piece of board or canvas in order to protect the floor from damage since the hand is driven downward and the broken pieces are slammed towards the floor.

#5. Avoid performing this break on bare ground, which would create too much of a cushion. A hard wood or concrete floor is most suitable. If the demo must be performed outdoors, a large sheet of plywood placed under the stansion blocks will aid in a successful break.

         A   B

#6. There are basically two methods to use when executing a "heavy break" (which refers to breaking concrete or cinder slabs with the bare hand).

    A. Stacked concrete refers to two or more slabs placed on top of one another. This method can be the most difficult, especially if the instructor has underestimated the ability of the person attempting to make the break. This break becomes almost impossible when the height of the stacked slabs nears the halfway measure (in length) of a single slab. For example: if the slab is 14 inches long and each slab stacked is one inch thick, the break becomes extremely difficult after the sixth slab is stacked on the others, which means that the stack is six inches high near the halfway mark.

    B. Spaced concrete means that after the first slab is placed upon the stansions, each slab thereafter has a one inch by one inch or one inch wide by one inch high by seven inches long wooden spacer at both ends. Now, one might say that "spacing each slab" will make the break easier. This question can be answered with a yes and no. It is easier to break because less "downward force" is needed to crack all the slabs, but at the same time, when one measures the amount of concentration needed on the focus point (center of both the top and bottom slabs) and the greater amount of speed which is necessary to enable the hand to carry through all the other slabs striking the bottom slab as hard as he strikes the top one, it is not easier.

#7. You should never attempt to break concrete or cinder slabs being held by hand. The risk of injury to the eyes, face, arms or feet when the broken pieces go flying to the floor is very high.

RULES TO FOLLOW BEFORE BREAKING BRICKS

#1. As in wood and concrete material, there are many different types of bricks, perhaps more varieties of bricks than anything else. Precautions must be taken in determining the type of bricks that one wishes to break while performing at a public demonstration. A finely ground, sand pressed brick is recommended. The authors' favorite was a name brand called "Clippert". Unfortunately they are no longer made, but there are many other brand name red house bricks that can be purchased which will serve the purpose just as well.

#2. Never purchase bricks that have been baked or scientifically hardened. The instructor should look for the old fashioned type farm house red brick. Within the last decade there has been a great demand for the old brick face type decor and many manufacturers have gone back to making bricks the original way, which is a mixture of a certain type of ground sand or clay pressed in a 2½" deep x 3½" wide x 8" long form and then left to bake in the sun. Some companies have their name stamped in the middle.

#3. It is said that if you clang two bricks together, the one that has the dullest ring is the easiest to break. This author uses that method but stresses that it only works about sixty percent of the time. A house brick has been a challenge to a karate Black Belt for more than 500 years, and even to this day, there is no absolute way to guarantee that a brick will break.

In addition to a little luck in choosing the right brick, the following factors must be present for a successful break: 1) Most important, the proper conditioning of arms, wrists and hands. 2) Concentration and focus. 3) The proper amount of body weight shifted at the precise moment the hand is at its maximum speed.

The author has estimated that it takes approximately 250 pounds of pressure to break one red house brick. Remembering that the weakest point of any object is in the center, the author can recall many times when a brick he struck broke less than two inches from the end; then there have been the times when a brick has broken exposing the razor sharp edges (almost the effect of a broken bottle), cutting the hand and wrist; and then there have been the times when the brick would not break at all, even when struck by a large hammer. This is why the breaking of a house brick should be left to the more experienced and highly skilled student or instructor. Such a break is indeed a challenge and should not be taken lightly. Successfully breaking one or more house bricks is perhaps the most dramatic expression of "hidden power" that the human body could ever expose, and it should be given the utmost respect and appreciation by participants in the art.

Breaking a house brick using a Ridge Hand technique.

Master Instructor Brenda Sell proves that women are not always the weaker sex breaking her first house brick at a demonstration in South Dakota.

House bricks on fire.

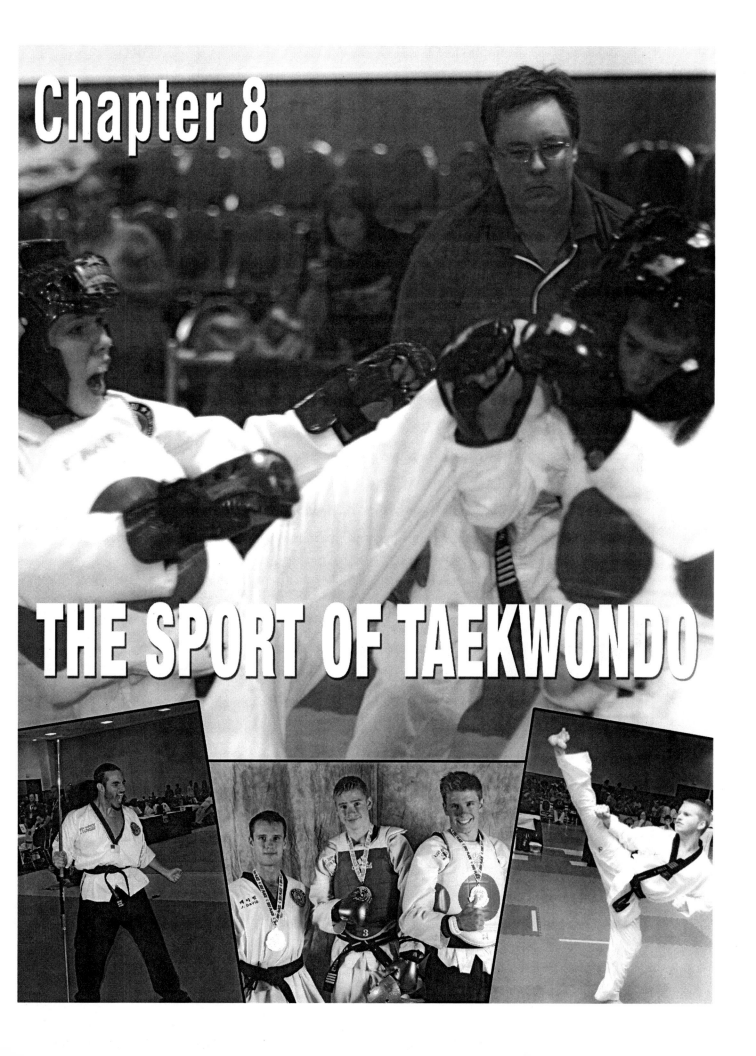

History to Current Times

EARLY HISTORY

Organized competition (sports) related to military combat (martial arts) have been a fabric of human culture for thousands of years in Asia, Africa, Europe, and the America's. The Ancient Olympic Games in Greece were contests of skills related to military combat, such as boxing, wrestling, pankration (mixed martial arts), armored foot racing, and chariot racing. The Roman Empire enjoyed a bloodier version of the Greek games, often held in large arenas (coliseums) as warriors known as Gladiators, fought to the death, amongst a cheering crowd. During the European Middle Ages and Renaissance Period, the "Tournament" became a popular spectator sport amongst the nobles, as they watched their champion knight's joust. In feudal Japan, sumo (a style of wrestling) matches were held in honor of the emperor. The champion was embraced as a national hero, evidenced in 500 year old scrolls and paintings. The All-China Wushu" (meaning martial art) Association was created in 1958 by the People's Republic of China. It has become a national sport, deriving its modern style from the many forms of traditional Chinese martial arts tracing back 3,000 years. The founder of Kodokan Judo, Sensei Jigoro Kano (1860-1938), introduced the art as a sport during the 1932 Olympic Games in Los Angeles (it later became a medal sport in 1964). Sensei Gichin Funakoshi (1868-1957) the founder of Shotokan Karate originally did not include sparring or "kumite" as part of his training, (he once said "There are no contests in karate.") instead he focused on "kata" (forms) and its applications. A former student of Sensei Funakoshi, Master Masutatsu "Mas" Oyama (1923-1994) founded Kyokushinkai, which taught stand-up, full contact kumite. Today the largest sport karate organization is the World Karate Federation (WKF) which formed in 1990, combines both kata and kumite competitions.

In 1971, President Chung Hee Park of South Korea announced that Taekwondo would become the national sport of Korea. Then, in 1973, the Kukkiwon was founded in Seoul Korea, becoming the world headquarters of Taekwondo. Under the Kukkiwon, the World Taekwondo Federation (WTF) was founded to oversee the competition aspects of Taekwondo as an international sport. On May 28, 1973, the WTF and Chung Do Kwan aligned with Kukkiwon. Sr. Grandmaster Woon-Kyu Uhm, is currently the President of the Kukkiwon and World Chung Do Kwan.

KUKKIWON

The Kukkiwon is the World Taekwondo Association Headquarters. It serves as the sole registry and determination of international certification for Black Belt (Adult Dan/Degrees & Children Poom) promotion throughout the world. It is the Kukkiwon which researches, designs, develops, and modifies the curriculum for this genuine martial art called "Taekwondo". The Kukkiwon decides what the requirements for promotion are, and if questions such as poomse interpretation are involved, then the Kukkiwon has the final say. When a candidate is promoted to a Black Belt rank, they receive a certificate, identification card, and a registration number from the Kukkiwon.

WTF

The World Taekwondo Federation (WTF) serves as the current International Federation for purposes of communicating with the International Olympic Committee (IOC). Currently, the WTF regulates all aspects of Olympic style sparring competition for Taekwondo and hosts the World Taekwondo Championships. The WTF certifies International Referees and conducts International Referee training and institutes the changes, if any, to the competition rules.

THE OLYMPIC GAMES

The World Taekwondo Federation was officially recognized by the International Olympic Committee (IOC) in 1980 to be considered as an Olympic sport. Taekwondo debuted during the Summer Olympic Games in 1988 as a demonstration sport hosted in Seoul, South Korea. Prior to that, Judo was the only Asian martial art venue in the Olympic Games. In 2000, Taekwondo became an official medal sport during the XXVII Olympiad, Summer Olympic Games in Sydney, Australia.

Other Olympic sports such as Track and Field, Gymnastics, and Swimming demonstrate the different facets of their sport by competing in several events; Olympic Taekwondo is allowed only one event, *sparring*.

Olympic Taekwondo is divided into four weight classes for men and for women, (half the number of weight classes used in Taekwondo World Championships). Taekwondo Kyorugi (sparring) at the Olympic Games is a single-elimination tournament to decide the gold and silver medals. There is a repêchage (French word meaning re-fishing) round among all contestants who lost to the two finalists. The two winners of the repechage finals are awarded the bronze medals. Matches consist of three two-minute rounds with a one-minute rest period between rounds, contested on a 10m x 10m (32.8ft x 32.8 ft) matted flooring. The match is decided by four corner judges and a center referee. The athletes are required to wear WTF approved equipment which includes a dobok, along with a chest protector (hogu), open face vinyl head gear and cloth or vinyl padded shin/instep protector and forearm guard, mouth guard, and supporter cup (for males). Electronic scoring equipment that is built into the chest protector is also being implemented.

Matches are scored by awarding a point for each legitimate blow and deducting a point for each penalty. Legal scoring areas are the hogu and head gear from the ears forward to the face and top of the head. Punches only (all other hand strikes are illegal) are allowed to score to the hogu (1 point), and kicks to the hogu are also scored as one point, while kicks to the head or face are scored two points.

USCDKA SANCTION TOURNAMENT CIRCUIT

The development and evolution of our USCDKA Sanctioned Tournament System has quite a heritage and goes back nearly 50 years with my own personal experience as a Student, Instructor, Master, International Referee, Grandmaster, and as a Kwan'Jang! I wish to begin this journey as I take you back to the early 1960's when modern-day Taekwondo started to evolve into a sport. That just happened to be the time when I was one of the very few foreigners in Korea that progressed in my martial arts training. I took my training so seriously that I took on the challenge of being a "Pioneer Competitor"! I was a newly promoted Black Belt at that time. Fortunately, the era that I was familiar with during those early years of training we now call the "Blood Sport era" (referring to the movie) was on its way out. Many schools at that time still taught "full contact" philosophy, including my school in Osan, Korea. It was fact that all other martial arts disciplines, called toe'chongs/schools) in Korea respected Chung Do Kwan for its power techniques. Why? Because the systems of teaching this ancient form of Taekwondo (Karate) did not believe in "pulling the punches!" There was much contact, especially in what was then called "Tae Soo Do Chung Do Kwan." The training was hard and rigorous. Very strict codes were in place, and when they were broken, severe discipline was enforced. The sparring sessions were brutal and, at times, quite vicious. Full contact was common. From this mind-set, tournament rules would soon be established. In 1963, I had the honor of being the only foreigner to compete in the first national tournament in Seoul, Korea. No one below the rank of black belt was allowed to experience such training. Chung Do Kwan was known to be the toughest Korean martial art, since the word control was only used when flesh met flesh or parts of the uniform touched the opponent's uniform. Only at that time was the aggressive force stopped and/or controlled while sparring. As a Black Belt student and competitor, I personally experienced those powerful blows that almost traumatized my body; I felt that awesome adrenaline rush; I bled from the nose, tasted blood in my mouth, and I have had my bell rung many times, but I also returned the favor quite often. For protection to our front torso, we wore very flimsy, bamboo chest protectors that was like wearing a thick sweat shirt; it didn't protect much; ribs were still being broken, kidneys were being ruptured, and lungs were being pierced with rib fragments. I watched my teammates being knocked out and heard their heads hit the concrete floor like dropping a bowling ball! Feeling like I was fighting for my life, I fought Korea's best, the champion of all the universities. No, I didn't win, but I felt happy being able to get a few good shots in before the end of each round, then walk out of that arena and not be carried out like so many others. Even though I was honored to have played a role in history as I personally experienced this primitive combat sport, my primary goal at that time frame was to study hard for my Master's Degree. My dream was to create a teaching profession, something unheard of during that era. While I was training hard in Korea, the now famous Chuck Norris, Joe Lewis (not the boxer) and Super-foot Bill Wallace were getting a name in the Karate tournaments in America. Karate uniquely adapted a scoring system similar to Judo competition. Judo was the first martial art that was officially recognized as a spectator sports event shortly after its origin, 100's of years ago, but the approval put Judo on the world map as an Olympic sport making it an international competitive event. I remember between my USAF tours to Korea, in 1964 and 65; I was stationed at Vandenberg AFB in California. I was a 2nd degree black belt in Chung Do Kwan, but Taekwondo had yet to make its debut in America, so I trained in Kodokan Judo. For a student to become a Judo brown belt, my Judo instructor required his students to compete in at least three tournaments, winning a medal in all three. I can remember it just like it was yesterday; prior to one of our Judo school's competitive meets, a Japanese Karate Instructor, named Hidetaka Nishiyama, who had a school in Los Angeles, hosted an exhibition Karate tournament with about ten students. I found it to be quite interesting, since Chung Do Kwan was closely related to the Shotokan Karate system (founded by Sensei Gichin Funakoshi). They used a similar scoring system as they did in Judo tournaments. The system used by Judo contestants, was called the "Flag System." It was a scoring system used in Japan for both Judo and Karate championships and became famous throughout that nation. I immediately realized this system to be much safer, more spectator friendly, and it also allowed all colored belt ranks to compete and not just Dan (Black Belt). This was totally opposite from my experiences in Korean competition. The Judo Flag System for scoring at a tournament required four judges, one in each corner of the 20m x 20m square matted ring, that was marked off on the floor. The most experienced was a center referee who controlled the match at all times. Each corner judge held a red flag in his right hand and a white flag in his left hand. Rather than called by name, each contestant was declared as "red or white". When contestant red applied a technique that was deserving of a score, any number of the corner four judges raised the respective flag and shouted "Ippon!" meaning "Point Scored!" The match was stopped and confirmed by the center referee, who then counted the number of officials that raised the same colored flag. If three or more of the same colored flags were raised, the contestant wearing the same colored flag on his belt (tied to his belt in the rear) was awarded the required points. An opponent can score a full point (Ippon) for a clean foot sweep or a mat-pin; half a point (Wazari) for controlling his opponent on the mat for more than one moment, or two full points for a clean perfect throw over the thigh, hip, or shoulder. I was not the only one that found this early-age karate tournament extremely exciting; the crowd roared with each technique that was delivered. The sport of Judo scoring system is still used today. As a result of that very event, which was also televised in 1964, Karate tournaments met the approval of sports enthusiasts not only in the U.S., but also throughout the world. I was honored to witness it and meet Master Nishiyama who later became the author of "Karate – Empty Hand". His book was extraordinarily similar to what I was taught during my early years in Tae Soo Do Chung Do Kwan in Korea. In 1967, while building my own chain of schools and establishing the

U.S. Chung Do Kwan Association (USCDKA), in Trenton, Michigan, I began to develop my profession as a Korean Karate instructor, thus the USCDKA was born! I am certain that God had His hand in it, since I had nothing and no one to guide me. One thing for certain, "I quickly realized that I had to tone down that hard-core training in order to gather enough students to make a living!" This forced me to develop a new free style sparring teaching philosophy. I refined a "control system" while sparring that was taught during my training as a student in Korea. This original system was only used in Chung Do Kwan schools, where contact was made with no attempt to deliberately injure an opponent. You must remember, that this was an era before the invention of safety hand and foot gear. This teaching principle prevented the most serious injuries while free style sparring. It demanded a tremendous amount of concentration and focus while performing the "Art" of one-step spar and the "Art" of free style sparring. This special system of teaching encouraged kids, boys and girls, and even women to join classes at my schools. During those early years in Korea and in the U.S., there were no children or women students. Since we wore no gear until the early 80s, my sparring system prevented injuries and forced all students to develop a very strong sense of self- discipline as they controlled each blow while showing the utmost respect to one another! I called it the "USCDKA Controlled Contact System". It was also during this era that I created the "USCDKA Four Point System" for tournament competition. This system produced tournaments that flourished throughout my region which was adapted by the AAU Taekwondo Tournament Committee in 1990 (a modified version is still used today). For many decades our students, family members, and spectators enjoyed the awesome excitement of competing in and witnessing hundreds of local, state, regional and national tournaments events. It was indeed a safe zone for students of all ages to test their skills in Taekwondo/Karate. The USCDKA soon developed a wonderful name and reputation in the tournament circuit. Since other Taekwondo/Karate tournaments took fewer precautionary measures to limit injuries than we did, injury rates were extremely high. Soon, USCDKA members were encouraged to be very selective in the tournaments they chose to compete in. Eventually, most of our schools either competed in association sponsored tournaments or not at all. Some of our Chartered Schools still compete in selected tournaments outside the USCDKA circuit. But, students are not allowed to compete in tournaments without their Sr.Instructors approval for safety and accountability reasons.

In 1979, after relocating our USCDKA headquarters from Ann Arbor, MI to Lakeland, FL, our local tournament involvement lightened as we began to rebuild our infrastructure and school charter memberships on a national scale. For many years, Grandmaster (G/M) Brenda Sell had a desire to form a USCDKA national tournament circuit. G/M Sell recalls her early years in training, "*I competed in tournaments for many years. I personally benefitted from every tournament, win, lose, or draw. I loved challenging myself to be the best I could be, working on developing technique, timing, and perfection for each event. The pressure and discipline forced me to continue and push through my insecurities and immaturity. I believe my involvement in tournaments helped shaped me into who I am today. My desire over the years was to provide a sanctioned USCDKA tournament where students could come together and compete with each other in a safe, secure, friendly, family environment. I want our USCDKA family to obtain the same benefits from competition that I did.*"

This renewed strong desire led her to put together a team to develop the dream. Soon, a system was developed and courses that certify all judges and referees. Her efforts proved to work extremely well and took hold with the debut of her "1990 Brenda J. Sell Classic!" Celebrating her 20 years of training. It was terrific success! With the growth of our schools in more that 30 states and in recognition of the USCDKA's 40th year of operation, we officially had our 1st USCDKA National Championship in 2007! Using our all new USCDKA 5-Point Lead System" formulated by our Lady President (G/M Brenda Sell) and her tournament team, that event was so perfectly run it was nearly "flawless", a word unheard of when organizing such a huge, competitive event. The 2007 National Championship officially kicked off the tournament circuit season, which begins immediately following the National Championship and ends at next year's National Championship.

The U.S. Chung Do Kwan sanctioned tournaments provide a safe, secure, friendly, family environment for members only. All competitors show a current USCDKA membership I.D. card in order to register to become a contestant. The friendly family environment has returned. We are once again a "safe zone" for all our students of all ages.

USCDKA Sanctioned Tournament Types

The USCDKA Sanctioned Tournament is divided into four categories, Local (Class D), State (Class C), Regional (Class B), and National (Class A). The USCDKA Sanctioned Local Tournament is an introduction phase, where an athlete learns the rules, and etiquette fundamentals necessary to succeed in the sport of Taekwondo. The Sanctioned State Tournament is a development phase that allows an athlete to utilize his/her fundamentals to acquire an understanding of the skills, techniques, strategies and tactics that are necessary to be successful in "Championship" matches. The USCDKA Sanctioned Regional Tournament is the high performance phase, where an athlete is expected to display a level of instinctive awareness and to understand the various tactical, technical, mental, physical and physiological components that are necessary to be a "National Champion" in competition. The Regional Tournament serves as a performance marker for athletes to qualify for the Nationals. The USCDKA Sanctioned National Championship Tournament is the "World Class" competition where an athlete displays an exceptional understanding of the sport and the mastery of the skills and techniques, with incontestable situational responsiveness, a sense of timing that enhances the execution of strategies and tactics in match competition on the national stage.

The USCDKA "Quest for A Champion" Point System allows athletes from each division to compete for the top ten competitors based on overall competition points earned throughout the tournament season and the winner is determined at the end of the Nationals. USCDKA Sanctioned Tournament Competitors have the opportunity of earning, state and national titles through the USCDKA system. In addition, USCDKA ratings will be posted on the website for each tournament season. Competitors will have double recognition through their involvement in sanctioned tournaments. A competitor that places 1st, 2nd, or 3rd in the National Championship, is entitled to wear the Official USCDKA National Champion Uniform during all USCDKA Sanctioned Tournament events. (All ranks and all ages). Points are awarded based on the Tournament Rating, participation and placement as follows:

Tournament Rating	1st place	2nd place	3rd place	Pre-registration	Participation points (per division entered)
4.0 Class D: Local Tournament	30	20	10	10	10
3.0 Class C: State Tournament	60	40	20	10	20
2.0 Class B: Regional Tournament	90	60	30	10	30
1.0 Class A: National Tournament	120	80	40	10	40

USCDKA Sanctioned Tournament Types

Poomse (Forms) & Keibons (Stationary Patterns)

Every competitor will be graded on a scale from 5.0 to 10.0. The average starting score for Poomse & Keibon competition is 7.0. Out of the 5 scores given per form or keibon, the highest and lowest scores will be taken out and the three remaining scores will be added to make the final score. In the event of a tie, the high and low scores will be added back in. If the tie is still not broken, the contestants will both perform in front of the judges who will declare the winner by raising their right or left hand. If for some reason the competitor must restart their form, whether it be due to nervousness or lack of memory, each judge shall subtract 1 full point from the final score. Competitors will be judged based on the following criteria:

Lines, Angles, Focus, Power, Precision, Enthusiasm, Posture, Technique, Memorization, Customs, Courtesies, Respect, and Confidence.

(Special consideration will be given to competitors under 6 years old.)

FORM COMPETITION TIPS

1. **Good Components Found in Form Champions:**
   - Lines, angles and joint adjustments (LAJA)
   - Power
   - Focus
   - Timing

2. **Common Attributes that would raise the score:**
   - Good Power
   - Good focus
   - Good timing
   - Good memorization
   - Precision of technique
   - Flexibility
   - Confidence
   - Attention to detail

3. **Common Penalties that would lower the score:**
   - Poor Stances
   - Poor Power
   - Poor Focus
   - Poor timing, hesitation
   - Loose fists on hips
   - Improper foot position
   - Elbows "winging" out
   - Shoulders not aligned
   - Eyes looking at the floor
   - Poor memorization

Any competitor who performs a poomse or keibon outside of their allowed range, will be disqualified from the competition.

During the competition, competitors will be expected to have good posture by sitting upright, have good body language by looking interested while the other competitors are performing, and have good expression by being pleasant and supportive.

All final decisions and interpretation of rules shall rest as the responsibility of the Tournament Director.

To find more information on the USCDKA Sanctioned Tournament Rules, visit www.uscdka.com.

Explanation of USCDKA 5 Point Lead Sparring & One Step Sparring

SPARRING: USCDKA 5 POINT LEAD

- Match time: One Round, 1.5 minutes. Time is stopped to confirm each point. Contestant must have at least three votes from the five ring officials to confirm the same point.
- Contestant with a 5-point lead or has the most points at the end of the match wins.
- Controlled (light) contact to head. - No contact to back of the head.
- A tiebreaker round will be held in the event of a tie. The first contestant to score a point wins.

SCORING TECHNIQUES:

- All traditional kicks should be recognized.
- One point when kick is placed in frontal portion of the body and flanks, between belt line and shoulders. (No points to the back area.)
- Two points for any controlled kick to the head. NOTE: Contact to headgear and face is allowed, slight touch ONLY! For lower ranked and younger (12 years and under) students, points will be scored for close contact as well as light contact.
- Higher ranked belts require more precision.
- Scoring is allowed from the ears forward, including the face.
- No contact is allowed to back of head.
- All techniques must be fully extended and controlled.
- Closed fist punches ONLY! Scoring area will be frontal portion of the body and flanks, between belt line and shoulders. (Backfist and chops are not scoring techniques).
- Partially blocked techniques do not qualify as a point.

NOTE: Faking with hands to the face is allowed, but contact will call for a ½ point warning or a full-point deduction.

SPARRING COMPETITION TIPS

1. **Good Components Found in Sparring Champions**
   - Endurance
   - Speed
   - Focus
   - Mobility
   - Combinations

2. **Common Attributes that would raise the score:**
   - Kicking to the body (Chest Protector)
   - Punching to the body (Chest Protector)
   - Kicking to the head (Legal target area)
   - Positioning in the ring for better visibility to judges
   - Loud Giyup (draws attention and shows aggression)
   - Sportsmanship

3. **Common Penalties that would lower the score:**
   - Kicking to the back
   - Kicking below the belt
   - Punching to the face
   - Holding
   - Running out of the ring
   - Pushing

SPARRING GEAR REQUIREMENTS (for USCDKA 5 Point Lead System):
All students must have a clean uniform and belt. Headgear, mouthpiece, chest protector and safety punch and kicks will be required for all competitors (in some regions, foot gear requirements vary slightly). Groin protection is REQUIRED for male competitors. Shin guards and forearm guards are optional

To find more information on the USCDKA Sanctioned Tournament Rules, visit www.uscdka.com.

SPARRING MATCHES AND SET-UP:

The competition point system for all tournaments shall consist of a single elimination. The "Bye System" shall be used at all tournaments, which guarantees four semifinalists. All byes shall be awarded during the first round of competition. The only exception will be in the case of only 3 competitors in free sparring. If the person who won the bye loses to the person who won the first round, the person who was awarded the bye will then be required to spar the person who lost to the 1st place champion.

We, the leaders of the USCDKA, must continue to instill the USCDKA "Controlled Contact System" in all our teaching philosophy! The method used to teach our students to score the points but without any intentions of inflicting serious pain or injury is indeed an "Art Within an Art"! To find more information on the USCDKA Sanctioned Tournament Rules, visit www.uscdka.com

ONE STEP SPARRING:

- Competitors will be paired based on Rank, Gender, Age, & Weight.
- Each competitor will perform 1 one step sparring technique at a time.
- After both competitors have performed 1 one step each, the judges will decide which competitor won that round.
- This will continue for a total of three rounds.
- The competitor who wins the match will be the one who won the most of three rounds.
- Competitors must compete using selections from the 20 one step sparring techniques demonstrated in the Forces of Taekwondo textbook.

The criteria for scoring One Step Sparring Competition will be as follows:

Proper Challenge, Proper Accept, Correct one step sparring routine, Striking on the striking line and intended target, Control, Proper stances, Giyup, Proper application of techniques, & Posture

ONE STEP SPARRING COMPETITION TIPS

1. **Good Components Found in One Step Sparring Champions**
    - Energetic
    - Focused
    - Determined

2. **Common Attributes that would raise the score:**
    - Good stances
    - Good power
    - Good focus
    - Good stances
    - Good challenges and accept

3. **Common Penalties that would lower the score:**
    - Poor power
    - Poor memorization
    - Poor focus
    - Poor challenges and accepting
    - Not striking on the striking line
    - Hesitation
    - Poor stances
    - Loose fists

CHUNG-DO XTREME

During the spring of 2005 at the U.S. Chung Do Kwan Leadership Conference in Lakeland Florida, we unveiled another historic event - CHUNG-DO Xtreme Forms and Weapons Training Curriculum! Combining traditional martial art techniques along with high energy gymnastics and acrobatics, the USCDKA once again pioneered another element of CHUNG-DO for the serious tournament competitor. World Class Extreme Martial Arts Champion *Daniel Sterling* in collaboration with USCDKA Headquarters has put together an unprecedented video series from beginner to advanced that will challenge any USCDKA student and Black Belt regardless of age.

CHUNG-DO Xtreme is <u>extenuating the basics</u>. The forms should display a continuity of power, finesse, fluidity, realism, focus, inspiration, harmony, integration, and unity of movement. It does not replace the "Traditional" USCDKA forms. All USCDKA students ARE REQUIRED to learn and practice their current rank material BEFORE beginning CHUNG-DO Xtreme training.

CHUNG-DO XTREME COMPETITION REQUIREMENTS
Eligibility Requirements
1. The competitor must be a member in good standing with the USCDKA and with a USCDKA chartered school and have permission from their Instructor.
2. The competitor MUST compete in Traditional Forms.

Clarification: As the popularity of Xtreme Martial Arts has grown over the past years, it is important that we do not neglect the traditional martial art skills that have been passed down from generation to generation. This helps ensure the proper technique, lines, angles, and joint adjustments are being developed and perfected.

3. Form and Rank Eligibility: (See website for current rules.)
    a. Beginner Students are only allowed to compete with Form #1
    b. Intermediate Students are allowed to compete with Forms #1 or #2
    c. Advanced Students are allowed to compete with Form #1, #2, or #3
    d. Black Belt Students are allowed to compete with any of the Extreme Forms.

Uniform Requirements

CHUNG-DO Xtreme competitors may wear any of the following approved uniforms:
1. An approved USCDKA traditional uniform with USCDKA logo on the back (sleeves cannot be rolled up)
2. A chartered school's traditional white uniform with USCDKA patch on left chest (sleeves cannot be rolled up)
3. Official USCDKA National Champion uniform (sleeves cannot be rolled up)
4. Official USCDKA Xtreme uniform

Clarification: Advantages of wearing the Official USCDKA Xtreme uniform is the lack of long sleeves, which can interfere with weapon performance getting snagged during a transition. It also gives judges a better view of the quick change-ups of hand techniques.

Weapons Requirements

After inspecting the weapon, Tournament Officials retain the right to refuse a weapon for competition due to safety concerns. Tournament Officials may stop the competitor if the performance becomes reckless and threatens injury to the competitor or by-standers.

The following approved weapons may be used to compete during CHUNG-DO Xtreme Competitions:
1. Kamas – Sizes 8", 10" or 12" (No sharp edged blades or straps allowed)
2. Bo (staff) – Sizes 3' to 6' 6" (Staff should be no more than 6" shorter or taller than a competitor's height).
3. Nunchakus – Sizes 10", 12" chain or rope (Home-made, ornamental, or protruding elements are not allowed)

To find more information on the USCDKA Sanctioned Tournament Rules, visit www.uscdka.com.

USCDKA Poomse & Keibon Strategies

Mastering the basics is the most important element of your poomse (including keibon) training. Regardless of your rank, your basics should look sharp. Practicing poomse without the basics is like trying to build a house without first laying the foundation. Once you have mastered the poomse basics, add these training methods listed below to your practice routine. Each method has its own specific purpose that will add an advantage over your competition.

1. <u>Concentration Method</u>. Perform each movement and technique slowly and deliberately with maximum tension, while maintaining proper form. Each movement is performed as if your body was refusing to do the movement and you must fight against it to complete the movement. This method is mentally and physically exhausting.
2. <u>Count Method.</u> Start each technique with a count. Then combine moves into one count. Finally perform the entire form from beginning to end non-stop without count.
3. <u>Pyramid Method.</u> Begin at chimbee, then perform bar one count one, and return to chimbee. Then perform bar one, count one and two, and return to chimbee. Repeat the process adding a count each time and return to chimbee until the entire form is completed. Focus on proper stance, power, balance, rhythm, during each count.
4. <u>Quick Method</u>. Complete the poomse as fast as you can while still maintaining proper form and power.
5. <u>Power Method.</u> Perform each movement and technique using maximum power at the moment of impact, while maintaining proper form.
6. <u>Backward Method.</u> Perform the poomse in reverse order from the end to the beginning (advanced).
7. <u>Mirror Image Method.</u> Start the poomse on the right side instead of the left or start on the left side instead of the right. It's great practice with a partner and for competition with a partner.

8. <u>Self Defense Method.</u> Add application to the poomse, with 2 or 3 attackers, according to a pre-determined scenario. Simulating reality but with perfect form.

How to Punctuate Your Poomse

When writing and using correct grammar, small punctuation changes can change the meaning of a sentence. Consider the sentence: *Woman without her man is an animal.*

- A woman may write: *Woman: Without her, man is an animal.*
- A man may write: *Woman, without her man, is an animal.*
- A headline writer may write: *WOMAN WITHOUT: her man is an animal.*
- A man named Herman may write: *Woman, without Herman, is an animal.*

Just as punctuation can change the meaning of a sentence, the same can be applied to poomse. Punctuating a poomse means for example holding a perfectly shaped front kick, for a brief second, or a loud GiYup, or a short pause between movements (to build expectation). Add your personal punctuation to the forms, but be careful not to change the pattern movements or their intended meaning.

Champion Tips

1. <u>Have a Good Backup Form</u>. Make sure you know the rules regarding ties. Some tournaments may require you doing a different form. Even if it isn't required, have a solid backup. If you can do a different form just as well as the first, you have a better chance of winning.

2. <u>Do not lose your concentration if you make a mistake</u>. Nobody is perfect. Some days are good days and some we try to forget. If you make a mistake, don't skip your rhythm or worse STOP! Keep going, add a technique or a step, and then get back into the form. The worst may be a ½ point deduction by a few judges, which is better than a 1 point deduction from all the judges for starting over.

3. <u>Do not be discouraged if you have to start over</u>. Just bow to the judges and ask if you can start over. Give your second try all the enthusiasm and effort of your first try.

4. <u>Your competitors are your peers</u>. You are competing against those in your same age group, belt level, and sometimes school. They are nervous too. During the match, they are the competition, you want to put on your game face and do the best you can to win. After the match, they are your peers, win or lose, the competition is over.

5. <u>Do not be intimidated by the judges</u>. They are people just like you that want each competitor to do his or her best. Do not be intimidated if they sit stone-faced, they are doing it out of respect for you.

Grandmaster Brenda Sell's Personal Form Competition Tips

Here are a few of my favorite tips that I personally have used to develop "Amazing Grace."

1. Practice Right. There is an old saying, "Practice makes perfect." This is only true if you practice the right things. If you practice wrong, you are embedding mistakes into your motor encoding. Practice, practice, practice. You really cannot practice too much when you are practicing correctly.

2. Little Things Make a BIG Difference. The difference between 1st, 2nd, and 3rd place is usually only half of a point or even tied. The little things will make the difference in your score. Little things, like a crooked back foot, a loose fist on the hip, or a low chamber could make a BIG difference in the outcome.

3. Practice in Front of a Mirror. If possible have mirrors on two walls that join in the corner. Practice your form full power by the count. Look at yourself in the mirror without moving anything except your eyes after each move. Correct the mistakes in your LAJA (Lines, angles, and Joint Adjustments) and start over. When you do the move the next time, think ahead and make the correction before you get to the move. (You don't want to wait until you get to the move to correct it, because you will be programming yourself to adjust after the move).

4. Focus on Power. The components of power encompass many of the components form, although not all of them. I truly believe that power covers a multitude of mistakes because the mistakes become minimal when you combing Power and LAJA.

5. Move with Confidence. Know your form inside out, upside down, and backwards. What I mean by this is that you should know your form so well that you can do it without having to think about the moves. The confidence this brings will help you to overcome potential mistakes and focus on form value.

USCDKA 5-Point Lead Sparring Strategies

Scoring Points While Not Being Scored Upon:

It sounds very simple. Score points and don't get scored on! Easier said than done, but a champion athlete understands the theory behind this very simple statement. There are many ways to score a point, many technical elements that, put together, will score a point. It is so tempting to focus on scoring that first point, that oftentimes we forget the importance of scoring the point strategically. Strategic sparring is more effective both short and long term. Points are made and matches are won by the smarter fighter.

- *Set up your points*. Anyone can kick, but few athletes can establish a "game plan". A game plan is where you lay a foundation, drawing the opponent in, essentially controlling your opponent's moves. So you can then execute the techniques you want to use without the threat of being scored upon. The smart athlete will learn to control the opponent's game without the opponent knowing he/she is being set up to be scored upon. Practice techniques that keeps you in control, using strategies that encourage the opponent to do exactly what you want them to do.

- *Engage only to score.* A common mistake athletes make is to engage at all costs. Of course, you cannot score if you don't engage, but engagement should be limited to scoring points and not just to be wildly punching or kicking. When you enter an exchange, it should be a precision strike. There should be a goal for the exchange and an exit strategy. In other words, each time you engage, you should get in, score the point, and get out, establishing distance and a comfort zone immediately upon ending the exchange. If you constantly engage for the entire fight, then it becomes nothing more than a kicking or punching contest, tiring yourself out without scoring a valid point. Develop the philosophy of kicking or punching with a purpose, while always being aware that the longer you engage, the more opportunity you give the opponent to land a point.

- *Create defensive strategies.* Defense means not getting scored upon. Defense is not running from the opponent or stepping out of the way. Defense is about running a smart game, establishing a tempo, and setting up strategies to prevent the opponent from scoring points in the process. Defense should be as precise as engagement. You can draw the opponent into complacency playing defense, only to strike when the opportunity arrives.

- ***Tactical Placement.*** It is important to maneuver your opponent into the most advantageous position for viewing and scoring of potential points. You should always position yourself and your opponent in a location that will provide optimal visibility to a majority of corner judges. This will maximize the potential for a point to be called.
- ***Keep it Simple.*** Go for the high percentage, safe kicks and leave the theatrics to others; use techniques that will not leave you vulnerable to being hit. Rely on your strengths and always be aware that your opponent is looking for any opening to score against you.
- ***Avoid unnecessary penalties.*** Penalties are the quickest way to lose a match. Once you have learned to set up points, engage only when necessary and with a purpose, establish defensive strategies, and hit and score without being hit and scored upon, why give up those hard fought points because of penalties? Learn how to manage the match by being aware of the rules of the game and be complimented by the rules and not aggravated by them. Pay attention to the officials calls in the ring and under what circumstances. Adjust to the rules, rule changes and rule applications.

Sr. Grandmaster Sell's Personal Sparring Tips

Here are a few of my favorite tips that I have personally given my students that have become Champions:

1. Don't look your opponent in the eyes. You shouldn't care what they look like. Look at his belly or waistline or the center dot on the chest protector.
2. Your kicks and hand technique should be hard and fast, but stop the force as soon as it touches a legal targeted scoring area.
3. Never let your guard down after bowing to your opponent.
4. Respect and accept all decisions of officials.
5. Don't show your emotions; if you are scared, hide it with a smile.
6. Be as courteous and respectful as you wish your opponent would be towards you.
7. Practice all martial arts customs and courtesies at all times.
8. If some part of your body hurts, ask for a time-out.
9. Be a Champion; act like a Champion; think like a Champion; feel like a Champion and you will become a Champion.
10. Here is my best and most famous tip: "Beat up your opponent's chest protector, not the opponent!

One-Step Sparring Tips

When practicing one-step sparring break each task down between attacker and defender.

Attacker Role

The attacker steps back and challenges with the right leg while executing a left low block over the left knee with the right hand chambered above the belt. When the defender gi-yups (shouts), the attacker must quickly step forward to a right square stance and deliver a right high punch to target #1.

Tips to remember:

- A common mistake is stepping back so that both feet almost become a straight line. This means you lose your balance and unable to move quickly into the punch. Ensure you are in a square stance during the challenge.

- Always make sure your punch has reaction force (push/pull) and is on target (upper lip).
- Always gi-yup (shout) when challenging, to let your opponent know you are ready to attack.

Defender Role

The defender evades the punch by moving and blocking and then performing a counter attack at the end. The most crucial part about defending is stepping, if you cannot step quickly with balance you will get hit.

Tips to remember:

- Most beginners when concentrating on the block totally forget stepping and stances. From your ready position try stepping quickly with balance left foot to right foot. After you are confident add on a block, then the strike. Practice each sequence one step at the time, then when you are technically correct you can add speed.
- Whenever blocking you should always block your opponent's wrist. The higher up the arm you make contact the harder it is to deflect their power.
- Always make eye-contact with your opponent when executing your techniques to maintain control and balance.
- Always gi-yup (shout) on your final counter attack to let your partner know you have finished.

CHUNG-DO Xtreme Tournament Competitor Tips

1. <u>Enthusiasm</u>. When your name is called, loudly acknowledge, and respectfully bow and present yourself to the judges. This sets a tone that alerts the judges that a motivated competitor is coming.
2. <u>Stances</u>. Keep your stances as low as they should be. Ensure your weight distribution and foot alignment are accurate. Excellent posture is important before and after your presentation.
3. <u>Rhythm</u>. Use correct rhythmic combinations. Try not to make your entire routine a blur. Stop for a second after each technique sequence to let the judges appreciate your solid stances, incredible balance, and perfect basics.

4. <u>Realism</u>. Remember you are fighting numerous imaginary opponents. Create the illusion of realism throughout your form.
5. <u>Facial Expressions</u>. Your facial expressions create the emotion in your form. It would be hard to take someone's form seriously if they smiled all the way through it. Keep your expressions serious and intensify your expression when you Gi-Yup.
6. <u>Eye Contact</u>. Look into the eyes of your imaginary opponents, not the floor. Eye contact is also a term for turning your head and looking in the direction you are about to move or strike.
7. <u>Work not Walk</u>. Work through the pattern, do not walk through it. If you merely walk through the pattern, you will have an average performance, whereas, if you work through the pattern, you will have a powerful performance that deserves recognition.
8. <u>Accuracy</u>. Make sure all techniques are within the striking lines and striking points.
9. <u>Power</u>. Move smoothly and deliberately, but execute the technique with maximum power and body tension. Strong kicks, punches and blocks are essential. It is better to have a strong low kick rather than a weak high kick. Do not give up power for flash.
10. <u>Balance</u>. Stumbling during a form is a major error. Demonstrate good balance during every turn, spin and jump.
11. <u>Symmetry</u>. Symmetry defined is beauty of form arising from balanced proportions (Lines, Angles, and Joint Adjustments). Poomse is very specific about LAJA in relation to the body. Pay close attention to your symmetry.
12. <u>Focus</u>. You must focus if you want your techniques to be accurate. Usually, when a person's eyes start to wander, he or she is unsure of the next move. Do not lose your concentration by distractions around you.
13. <u>Speed</u>. Even in a simple form, showing a quick combination of movements is important. Do not emphasize speed exclusively.
14. <u>Crisp Techniques</u>. Ensure your techniques are Snap, Crackle, and Pop. The arm, leg, or body should move from one position to the next as quickly as possible and should stop exactly in its next position.

15. _Flexibility_. If your flexibility is good, you will be able to perform difficult kicks with ease. Nothing is more exciting than watching someone throw a kick straight up with good execution and power.
16. _Perform for the back row_. Stage actors make exaggerated movements so the movements may be seen by people sitting in the last row of the theater. When doing your form, you should perform for the person sitting on the top row of the bleachers. When sweeping movements are required, make them very large sweeping movements; when a snap is required make it very snappy; when power is required, make it very powerful.

Develop a Tournament Plan

Having a game plan is a crucial part of any competitive training. It can make a huge difference in your results. Inconsistent preparation can lead to inconsistent performance. Establishing a tournament routine is essential for every athlete's training program. It creates a foundation which sets the tone for the entire competition. Some athletes think that they have an established routine, when in fact what they have is a ritual. A ritual is a set of behaviors based on superstition (i.e. a lucky t-shirt, or rubbing hands together, etc.) which has no relation to measured performance. An athlete that focuses on rituals is more concerned about doing those things correctly, rather than focusing on how it affects their performance. Having a routine is having an established plan of task-related behaviors, giving the athlete a sense of self control, stability and readiness. Developing a well planned routine can significantly reduce inconsistencies and enhance performance. Developing a tournament routine is broken into five phases, 1) weeks before the tournament, 2) day before the tournament, 3) tournament day, 4) immediately after the tournament, 5) days after the tournament. There are many types of pre-tournament routines; the following are just basic steps to get you in the right direction. Use these basic steps and develop what is right for you.

Weeks before the tournament

1. A tournament routine starts with doing some reconnaissance, a military term that means research.
   - Know the location of the tournament: the exact distance, time for travel, make appropriate reservations if necessary for plane, car, or hotel.
   - Expected weather conditions (pack appropriate clothes)
   - Detailed map of the tournament location and tournament flyer (downloaded from USCDKA website) and kept in a tournament folder.
2. Begin your tournament training program (using the training tips)
3. Prepare your tournament equipment
   - Have a ready made checklist. Check your uniform, sparring gear, weapons and repair or replace if necessary (it's a good idea to have a second set in case the original set is damaged prior to the tournament)
   - Pack your equipment in appropriate bags or cases

Day before Tournament

1. <u>Do not train</u>. Relax
2. Visualize yourself winning; see yourself actually in a match. Try to visualize the sounds, your feelings, your tactics, and most of all, your winning. If a negative visualization creeps in, stop, rewind to just before the negative, and start again. Repeat a short but inspiring personal slogan, mantra, or Bible verse, over and over in you mind to calm and center your thinking.
3. Do not change your eating habits except to eat plenty of complex carbohydrates for the evening meal. Avoid alcohol or caffeine.
4. Get 7-8 hours of sleep. If you must rise early to commute to the tournament, then go to bed earlier. If the tournament will involve a long commute, consider arriving the day before.

Tournament Day

1. Eat a light breakfast. Eat small snacks throughout the day (energy snacks) so digestion will not sap your energy when you are ready to compete. Keep yourself hydrated (water) throughout the day.

2. Arrive with plenty of time to take care of tournament business, such as registration, meetings, or weigh-in, and to allow you time get used to the environment, such as temperature, humidity and noise level.
3. Familiarize yourself with the arena. Know where your assigned ring is located and be near it as your event time approaches. Know where the nearest restrooms are located.
4. Time your warm-up so you will have a light sweat when your event time arrives.
   - Establish a preparation cycle; for sparring, hydrate, use restroom, don sparring equipment, warm-up, and stretch.
   - Keep moving to maintain you flexibility and focus.
   - Relax and cultivate your fighting spirit. Focus on the task at hand and reject all other thoughts.
   - Listen to your favorite music on your IPod or MP3 player (not too loud that you can't hear the announcements)
5. For sparring study your environment and opponents
   - Before you spar, know the environment: ring size; positions of judges; personalities of judges and referee; and how judges and referees score.
   - Study your possible opponents: their size/reach; how they guard and block; what stances they use; whether they are kickers, punchers, counter-attackers, or a combination; how they make eye contact; do they run from attacks, stand their ground, or rush in; do they move around a lot or do they stay basically motionless; do they attack with front or back foot or in combination; and are they basically right or left sided in their attacks.
6. When you are called to enter the ring, answer loudly, run to your position, and perform your poomse or spar as if everything depended on your winning.
7. Whether you win or lose, show good sportsmanship, run off the mat, relax and think about what you did wrong and how you can improve it the next time.
8. If you have to spar again, start the preparation cycle again. If you win, you may have to condense the cycle, so you are ready to spar again in short notice.
9. After the event is over, consult with other competitors, your instructor, your coach, or fellow students about how you may improve. Attend to any injuries and relax.

Immediately after the Tournament

1. If you lose, do not display outward anger or become a whiner. Every champion had to lose at least once. Accept it as a learning experience; begin by evaluating your plan and how you may have to make changes to improve your weaknesses before the next tournament. Do not leave the tournament to wallow in self pity or anger. Instead, stay to encourage and cheer on your teammates in their matches. That shows leadership!

2. If you win, accept the medal or trophy humbly as a reward for your hard work and effort. After the award ceremony, it is tradition to present the medal or trophy to your instructor. In some cases, they may hold it for you until the event is over, and in other cases, they may just congratulate you and give it back to you immediately. Thank them for their hard work in training you. Thank the other competitors for a well fought contest. Thank the judges and referee for their fairness in judgment. Relax, and begin making a mental plan on how to improve for the next tournament. Do not leave the tournament area to celebrate. Stay to learn by watching others as well as to encourage and cheer your teammates in their matches. Brag on their wins, but do not brag on your own wins.

Days after the Tournament

1. Go over the event; evaluate your actions and inactions. Solicit feedback from others about your performance. Do not question or reply, just listen and write down their critiques to use for your evaluation.
2. Begin to wind down. Relax and do relaxing things for a few days. Do not train.
3. After a few days, return to your training routine using all the things you learned to adapt your training towards improving your performance.

TOURNAMENT OFFICIALS

Good Sportsmanship is a top priority during all USCDKA Sanctioned Tournaments. The first tenet of Taekwondo is "Courtesy", and that is important to remember when interacting with tournament officials. Talking disrespectfully to an official or not following their directive is not acceptable. The manner in which you and your school are represented is far more important than winning or losing. Good Sportsmanship is also about respect – respect for oneself, for teammates and coaches, for your opponents, tournament officials and the game itself. Tournament Officials are there as volunteers to help the tournament run smoothly and therefore should be treated with respect. Even if it is a person you know and recognize, you need to treat them as an official, not as your instructor, parent, or neighbor, etc. They are expected to display a consistent, professional manner and attitude at all times. Tournament officials must also treat participants with courtesy and impartiality. During the competition Tournament Officials (Referee, Judges, Timekeeper and Scorekeeper) must not speak with anyone outside of their ring other than the Tournament Director and Chief Referee. Spectators are not allowed to coach from the sidelines, or opinionate to any of the Tournament Officials. In the event of a dispute over any Tournament Official or officials call, the process in the current rules must be followed. Any call made by the Chief Referee/Arbitrator and Tournament Director will be final.

Tournament Director Role and Responsibilities

- Ensures correct preparation is given for the tournament in consultation with the tournament organizing committee, with reference to competition area arrangement, the provision and deployment of all equipment, awards and necessary facilities (i.e. medical, refreshment, pro shop), event operation and supervision is safe, secure, friendly and family.
- Setting of divisions according to rank, age and gender
- Priorities are safety, fairness, and development of officials
- Maintains communication with Chief Referee/Arbitrator, Staging, Medical and Security.

Chief Referee/Arbitrator Role and Responsibilities

- Oversees and manages the Referees and Judges.

- Works as an assistant to the Tournament Director.

Referee Role and Responsibilities

- Poomse: The Referee oversees the judges, directs poomse performance and scores.
    1. The Referee calls for a simultaneous show of scores from judges.
    2. Confirms the scores with the Scorekeeper and reviews 1st, 2nd, and 3rd place scores.
    3. Announces 3rd, 2nd and 1st place winners.
    4. In the event of a tie (after the low and high scores have been entered), the competitors will perform the poomse simultaneously. The Referee and Judges point to the winner.
- Sparring: The Referee is responsible for all activities inside the ring
    1. Inspects competitors equipment
    2. Stops the match when Judges yell "Point"
    3. Calls for points and announces loudly if a point is awarded to the Scorekeeper (must have at least three confirmations including Referee).
    4. Stops the match when an infraction is committed, and calls a warning or penalty to the appropriate offender
    5. Maintains safety in the ring at all times
    6. Announces winner by holding competitors arm up high
    7. To disqualify a contestant for an infraction (must confirm with Chief Referee/Arbitrator and Tournament Director).

Judges Roles and Responsibilities

- Calls points for competitors when called by Referee by raising the score card or flag high for the Scorekeeper to see.

Timekeeper/Scorekeeper Roles and Responsibilities

- Keep accurate time and score during competition.

Coaching

Coaches play a vital role in providing students/athletes with the skills and knowledge needed to develop, improve and reach their goals. Coaches also have a major influence over participants' enjoyment of Taekwondo. It is essential that coaches provide students of all ages the best possible experience, ensuring their continued participation and development. Certified training as a coach is an important first step to ensuring that you are on the right track with your involvement. Through accreditation you will gain the credibility you deserve and participants will be more confident in the knowledge that a qualified coach is instructing them.

Coaching Skills

As a coach you will find that you need to develop many skills. These include:

1. Know how to communicate effectively with your athletes
2. Understand the learning process, training principles, and appropriate teaching methods (coaching styles)
3. Understand the capabilities and limitations of growing children
4. Advise athletes on safe training practices
5. Understand the causes and recognize the symptoms of over-training
6. Understand how to reduce the risk of injury to your athletes
7. Prepare training programs to meet the needs of each individual athlete
8. Advise athletes on their nutritional needs
9. Advise athletes on relaxation and mental imagery skills
10. Evaluate the athlete's competition performance
11. Provide feedback after competition is completed

In summary, tournaments are a learning experience, an opportunity to test your skills under stress, compete in a safe, secure, friendly, and family environment. It is an opportunity to meet old friends and make new friends. It doesn't matter if you win or lose, tournaments should be fun, if it's not, then you are doing something wrong.

Final Thoughts ....

DEVELOPING THE SPIRIT MAN
Brenda J. Sell

Deep inside of man there has always been quest for more power, searching to reveal the unknown, and ultimately tapping into a greater power source. In this section I will share the truths I have discovered that tap into this greater power source.

There are two distinct experiences in our Taekwondo career that forced me to look closer into the reality of the "Missing Element" necessary for true contentment in life.

The first experience happened at our school in Ann Arbor, Michigan. My husband and I were in the office between classes when a sloppy looking middle-aged man barged in with his teenage son. He was dressed in overalls that were very worn and wrinkled. He had not shaven for some time and looked like maybe he had a habitual drinking problem. The son was quite nervous and carried a chip on his shoulder that was a result of insecurities from the negative influence his father had on him. The two were from Detroit and had traveled to Ann Arbor to see us because thy heard about the results we were experiencing with troubled children through the disciplined and structured classes. We talked for a few minutes and the father began to show his anxiety. He said, *"Well, I'm leaving this blankety, blankety, x%#*^x with you. I've had it! He's yours!"* He then walked out of the office and building, literally leaving this young man on our doorstep! I can still see the look of this young man that day. His shoulders were slouched forward, he wore a black leather beret, blue jeans, a brown t-shirt and a jacket. His face was very stern, with his head lowered and looking through his eyebrows. He couldn't or wouldn't look you in the eyes. We helped set the young man up so that he had a place to stay and could train. He was an incredible student and a hard worker. Soon, as he developed a good self-image he began to develop into a leader. One day, he walked into the office and asked if he could talk to us about something very personal. As he opened up his heart, he explained *"something was missing."* You see, he had strengthened his body and his mind through his Taekwondo training, but there was still a void.

Years later, we found ourselves at a USCDKA Charter Member School in Indiana. The instructor was very well educated and had a good, successful Taekwondo school. When we finished teaching him and his students, we went to his office to talk. He wanted to know about the "deeper truths of martial arts." Like the experience we had earlier, he stated *"something was missing."* He was quite a bit more articulate, but he had the same concern, there was a void.

Over and over again we would see that when as our students moved into the black belt ranks they would declare *"something was missing."* At this level the black belts are in peak physical and mental condition. The training in Taekwondo pushes a person beyond what they think they are capable of doing. There is a saying, *"Winners are not Quitters, and Quitters are not Winners."* Quitting is not an option. Because of the discipline, focus, and concentration required to excel, these traits also improve the ability to think. Grades of school-age children almost always improve within six months. Adults are better able to cope with problems and stress. Both the body and mind are stimulated to peak performance during the years of intense training. However, time and time again, we would hear, *"somethings missing!"*

Man is a Spirit, the Lives in a Body, and Possess a Soul

The missing element in all of these cases was that their being was off balance. Balance is a key to life. The SPIRIT is the real you, the part of you that will live forever. Of the three components, the spirit is the most powerful. The BODY is our physical being. The SOUL comprises the mind, will, and emotions. Let's look at the creation of mankind according to the Bible. In the book of Genesis we discover that God created Adam out of the earth and formed a body for him to live in. God then breathed the breath of life into Adam bringing him to life by giving him a spirit. We see that Adam also had intellect, a free will, and emotions all of which are components of the soul. Looking at the New Testament we see in Hebrews 4:12 (ESV) that the spirit and soul are two different components. *"For the Word of God is living and active, sharper than any two-edged sword, piercing to the division of soul and spirit, of joints and of marrow, and discerning the thoughts and intentions of the heart."*

BODY

Take care of your body. Make a decision to be healthy and to develop habits to live a healthy lifestyle. Developing physical strength (in the body) is a science. It does not come by chance. It is **your** responsibility to keep your body fit. Take care of your body today and tomorrow it will take care of you.

FOOD: You are what you eat is a phrase we have heard for many years, but is worth repeating. A healthy diet is certainly one of the keys to a healthy body. Research shows that the healthiest diet is one with minimal amounts of sugar, salt, preservatives and additives as well as limited quantities of stimulants such as coffee and alcohol. While a fair but not overwhelming amount of meat may be beneficial, whenever possible, substitute fish or fowl. Your diet should be well rounded and foods should be eaten as close to their natural source as possible. This means fresh fruits and vegetables and drink plenty of water. Evaluate what you put in your mouth comparing the benefits and consequences to your health.

EXERCISE: Develop a regular program of exercise. Exercise is an essential ingredient to a healthy lifestyle. Develop an exercise program that fit you. It should be well rounded, practiced regularly and pleasurable. Being a martial art student, you obviously found a unique form of exercise. Stay with it as long as possible and practice at home. If you should discontinue your training, try to establish your own exercise program using methods taught to you during the time you were active. If you are not a martial arts student, find activities that will enhance strength, tone, flexibility and coordination while also improving respiratory, cardiovascular and mental functioning. Find a class or group that teaches you to stretch, breathe and carefully exert yourself. It is a proven fact that group orientated classes that are well structured and promote goal setting will keep your interest longer, providing lasting benefits.

REST: Take time out. Read and reflect. Whenever possible, take vacations and mini vacations. Block out periods of time when you can simply get away from your usual environment and routine to get refreshed. Don't become stuck in your own "dis-ease". Give your body a break.

SOUL

The soul is actually the mind, will and emotions. With the soul, man contacts the intellectual realm. It is said that we have not even tapped into the capabilities of our minds. We can develop our soulish realm by choosing what we feed it. Developing the soul not only includes feeding your mind, but protecting it from negative influences.

GUARD YOUR THOUGHTS: Protect your mind. Thoughts come and go, but thoughts unspoken die unborn. Realize that not every thought is your thoughts. Some thoughts come from experiences, others from what we see (television, internet, movies, activities, etc.), hear, taste, touch, and smell. Our senses are connected to our thoughts. Other times, thoughts may come that are in opposition to your core values.

What you feed grows, what you starve dies. Thoughts in themselves have no power over you. It's what you do with the thoughts that will determine your emotional state. The progression to action is:
1. Think it.
2. See Yourself Doing It.
3. Do it. (Live into the picture).

Guard your mind! Be careful what you feed it. Scientist has discovered that criminals thought about their crimes, saw themselves doing it and when they actually did it, it was natural. They already trained themselves to do wrong in their mind and the body responded. The same is true on the positive side. Choose the thoughts you mull over in your mind. Think about what you think about. You can only think about one thing at a time. What you think on eventually comes out of your mouth and is eventually put into action. Be careful of what you hear. Guard your mind! Get your mind quiet and feed your mind things that will strengthen your spirit, not your ego.

CHOOSE YOUR FRIENDS WISELY: Friends are a great influence on each other. Have you ever met two friends who even laugh the same? Many married people eventually think alike because they influence each other. Influence affects your soul.

SPIRIT The spirit is referred to as "the heart of man." The spirit is the real you, the part of you that lives forever. We know that man is a spirit; because he is made in the image and likeness of God and God is a Spirit. Out minds cannot grasp things in the spiritual realm. If you listen to your spirit, there's something that responds on the inside of you because your heart knows it's true. The spirit is the life-giving force; our body is the physical being; and the soul is the mind, will and emotions. Taekwondo will exercise the body and the soul, but when they are developed there is still a void because the spirit is still hungry. There is still "something missing!" How can we tap into the limitless power that exists in the spirit? Man must recognize that all strength, wisdom and understanding begins with knowledge of the Holy One, and that through a close walk with Him this vast potential can be obtained.

> *Consider this* ……..
> If the spirit is the life-giving force to our body, then it would follow that our strongest energy source comes from the spirit, rather than the body or soul?

SEARCH FOR SPIRITUAL TRUTH. The first step is desire. The Bible tells us, if we seek God we will find Him. Desire to know God, search for truth and He will make Himself real to you! You will discover that you are valuable to God, that your life has purpose, and that you are loved. Find out who you really are. Spiritual exercise is healthy. Search for spiritual truth. Be careful for there are two sides, the light and the dark. When you walk in the light you will never be misled for you can always see where you are headed. When you walk in the dark there will always be confusion and satisfaction is only temporary.

Let us take a moment to contrast the two.

Light	Dark
Conviction (way of escape)	Condemnation (no way of escape)
Leads or draws	Pushes away
Direction	Confusion
Peace	Turmoil (strife, discord, jealousy)
Faith	Fear

FOLLOW THE LIGHT. Jesus said, *"I am the way, the truth and the light, no man comes to the Father but by me."* The ONLY way to find the "missing link" is through a personal relationship with Jesus Christ. Being good and doing good things are fine, but they will not provide you with eternal life. You must be born-again. Until your spirit is "born-again" you cannot even see the Kingdom of God let alone live in it. A person who is not born-again (spiritually receiving God's spirit into your spirit) could not live in heaven because he does not have the nature of God in him to survive in heaven anymore than a fish could live out of water. So you see, it's not about what you do or how you behave, it's accepting God's provision for a relationship with you through His son, Jesus Christ.

TAP INTO THE SPIRIT. When a person accepts Jesus Christ as their Lord and Savior, they are actually making a commitment that God will now be the final authority or BOSS of their life. It's a total act of surrendering your rights to serve Him. When this happens, our spirit is born-again and the Holy Spirit of God takes residence in our spirit. The Spirit of God actually lives inside of us 24 hours a day, 7 days a week. He's always there. His role is YOUR personal helper, guide, and teacher. When you tap into the Holy Spirit, you tap into a new kind of power – the ultimate spiritual power. He will help you increase your sensitivity in the spiritual realm where God operates so that you can have a victorious life in every area.

MAKE A COMMITMENT TO RECEIVE FROM GOD. Romans 10:9,10ESV says *"If you confess with your mouth that Jesus is Lord and believe in your heart that God raised him from the dead, you will be saved. For with the heart one believes and is justified and with the mouth one confesses and is saved."* There are two parts described here: confessing with your mouth and believing in your heart. What are we confessing? That Jesus is Lord. Lord of what? Lord of your life. Lord is a strange term for some of us, but it simply means the final authority or boss of our life. We give up our life in exchange for His. This is crucial. People everywhere are giving up on life and even attempting to take their lives through suicide. Don't do it that way! Give your life over to Jesus and you will now have purpose and a future. He will not let you down. Everything you need He has provided for you. Believe in your heart means that you have made a commitment. This word believe is not just knowing, it means to cling to, adhere to, kind of like super glue, never letting go of the commitment in your heart to turn your life over to God.

AN INWARD CHANGE TAKES PLACE. 2 Corinthians 5:17 says: *"If any man is in Christ he is a new creature, old things are passed away, behold all things become new."* Our senses change. It's a spiritual experience. We know that it is not a change of mind because we still know the things we knew before. This part, the soulish realm has to be changed by "renewing our mind" with the Word of God, the Bible. The Bible is the textbook on life. It was inspired by the Holy Spirit and contains all of the answers to today's problems. How do we tap into the strength that is within the "inward man" or the "spirit of man"? Once we receive Jesus as our Lord and Savior, we must grow. Spiritual growth comes in many ways; prayer, Bible study, worship, church attendance, fellowship with other believers.

BECOMING BORN-AGAIN. The Bible tells us in John 3:3-8 that our spirits must experience a new birth in the same way our bodies do in the birthing process. When Jesus told Nicodemus, *"you must be born again,"* Nicodemus was in awe because he did not understand that Jesus was referring to the spiritual birth. Nicodemus wanted to know why Jesus possessed so much power and how he could attain it. He was looking at Jesus through the intellectual (soul) and physical (body) realm. Jesus replied, *"I tell you the truth, unless man is born of water (physically) and the Spirit, he cannot enter the kingdom of God. Flesh gives birth to flesh, but the Spirit gives birth to spirit. You should not be surprised by my saying, you must be born again."* NIV

To become "born again", one must fist accept the statement of John 3:16, *"For God so loved the world that He gave His only begotten Son, that whosoever believe in Him shall not perish but have everlasting life."* Romans 10:9 tells us that, *"if you confess with your mouth Jesus is Lord and believe in your heart that God raised him from the dead, you will be saved."* NIV

God is telling us there is hope, and that through the process of being "born again" we can do anything through Christ Jesus, as our source of strength. (See Philippians 4:13)

BE RESPONSIBLE AND LOYAL TO YOUR COMMITMENTS. One of the most difficult tasks that I can think of is to be loyal to your commitments. The Bible, John 10:10, talks about a thief who comes *"to steal, and to kill and destroy"*. The thief in the spiritual realm is Satan. Yes, Satan is real. What is it that he desires to steal, kill and destroy? What can we do about it? How do we overcome depression and suicidal tendencies?

God has a Master Plan for your life. A commitment always includes a cost or a price. Remember commitment is a personal choice that only you can make. There are many battles to be won, physically (body), psychologically (soul), and spiritually (spirit). The driving force is deep within your born-again spirit, by the Spirit of God. Satan's desire is to steal, kill and destroy that goal before it became a reality. Jesus goes on to say in that same verse (John 10:10), *"I have come that they might have life, and that they might have it more abundantly." 2 Corinthians 10:4 tells us: "The weapons of our warfare are not carnal, but mighty through God."* Ephesians 6:10-17 tells us that the toughest struggles we have in this life are not physical, but spiritual. God has supplied us with weapons that are referred to as "the armor of God." *"Finally, be strong in the Lord and His mighty power. Put on the full armor of God so that you can take your stand against the devil's schemes. "For our struggle is not against flesh and blood, but against the rulers, against the authorities, against the powers of this dark world and against the spiritual forces of evil in heavenly realms. Therefore pun on the full armor of God, so that when the day of evil comes, you may be able to stand your ground, and after you have done everything, to stand."* Then verses 14-18 explain what the armor of God consists of for every person who ha been born again. God will carry you through every trial as you put your faith in God. This kind of commitment is available to anyone who looks for it. Jesus says to us, *"Seek and ye shall find, ask and it shall be given, knock and the door shall be open."* Are you willing to pay the price? The choice is yours. Be responsible to yourself and loyal to your commitments. Relying on spiritual strength is the way to the "perfect peace" that is explained in Philippians 4:6 and 7, *"a peace of mind that passes all human understanding."*

ACTION STEP:
THE COMMITMENT TO DEVELOP YOUR SPIRIT

> **Man is a Spirit, that lives in a Body, and possesses a Soul**

We are all triune beings. In other words, every human being has three parts. We are spirit beings, who live in a body, and we communicate through our soul (mind, will, and emotions). For years, we counseled black belts who after training in Taekwondo for years, discovered they were "missing something." That something was their spirit seeking after God. In my own case, I discovered to grow strong spiritually; I needed to be "born again" (John 3:3). I also learned that to be born again, meant to receive Jesus Christ as my Lord and Savior (Romans 10:9-10). I had always believed in Jesus, but had never really given my heart and life to Him, and let me tell you that when I did, it was the most important day in my life. I was changed and became a new creation in God (II Corinthians 5:17). What I am referring to is not a religion-but a relationship, no rules and regulations, but freedom to be everything that God intended me to be.

> **A true master of the arts will seek a balance of spirit, soul and body.**

Jesus said *"For what shall it profit a man to gain the whole world, and lose his soul?"* (Mark 3:36). The Bible tells us that if we draw nigh to God, He will draw nigh to us (James 4:8). It is our prayer that as you meditate and study the Holy Scriptures and "Draw nigh" unto God, that you will experience His love, His forgiveness, and the free gift of eternal life through Jesus Christ. To help you develop a relationship with the Lord, we have listed some simple steps, known as the four "R's" of salvation, and a simple prayer for you to follow. If you follow these steps and say this prayer from your heart, you will become Born Again and will experience the "peace that passes understanding".

Realize that you are a sinner!
Romans 3:23 "For all have sinned and fall short of the Glory of God".
Repent of your sins!
1 John 1:9 "If we confess our sins, He is faithful and just to forgive us of our sins and cleanse us from all unrighteousness.
Receive Jesus into your life!
Romans 10:9-10 "That is you confess with your mouth the Lord Jesus, and believe in your heart that God raised Him from the dead, thou shalt be saved."
Release Jesus into your life!
Matthew 6:33 "But seek ye first the kingdom of God and His righteousness; and all these things will be added unto you."

SINNER'S PRAYER
PRAY THIS PRAYER FROM YOUR HEART:
Dear Lord Jesus,
I am a sinner. I believed that you died on the cross for me, and I ask you to forgive all of my sins. I receive you as my Savior and Lord of my life. Please take full control of my life and help me to be the kind of Christian that you want me to be, and as you have forgiven me, I also forgive everyone that has ever hurt me. Amen.